18⁰⁰

LOOKING FOR GOL

Looking for Gold

A Year in Jungian Analysis

Susan M. Tiberghien

DAIMON

ISBN 3-85630-550-5

Cover photo: "Maple Tree" by Michael Melford.

Contents

Foreword

Susan Tiberghien is a writer, a wife, a mother of six, a believer, with a laughter that keeps situations in perspective. I see her book as a writer's journey (but that is only a starting point), renewing faith by calling creation's trickle and flood from life's mysterious bedrock: the dream. An annealed beginner emerges from her months of exploration. Stronger, and in possession of her woman's voice, she charts steps of knowledge, purpose and no turning back.

Susan selects dreams from her Jungian analysis that pick up unconscious and soul material where one meets hunger and thirst. Opening her life to these lacks, we see her go through periods of disorientation, physical symptoms, and a suspension of disbelief. Waking hours often become like dreams. Her climb up a mountain that she has known with her family for thirty years, suddenly reveals a reality: she has been climbing it by strength of will, not from a deep inner pull. Fear, like a Biblical angel, grounds her, so that almost paralyzed, she has to crawl down, collapsing at the bottom. We follow the woman into her self and its seasons – the task so foreign to most of us – accompanied by her Virgil, the analyst Keller.

The material is dynamite. The raw magma in our mind, the stuff that connects us with the reality of life, and our own beginning and end, is so powerful that it cannot be taken in large doses or lightly. Once tapped, it flows and spills. Susan pans it for what she consciously wishes to know. Coaxing insights from dreams, she and Keller invite the independent signs to live incarnated in daylight.

Susan Tiberghien's year of work is thorough, passionate and round in shape. She made the time to devote herself to it, to speak to her inner spirits, to catch up after years and years of family and organizing things for others. She wrote these pages because we need voices that sound distances, showing where order and pattern play with information incredibly hidden to us. Susan is one acquainted with the invisible.

We are fortunate when someone is seized by the painful fervor of recording faith. In a world of no answers, Susan points to discarded resources in our human minds. Why did she transcribe how an analysis feels? Because she grew; this impelled her to share firsthand how she gained ground on our waking hours.

In an inspired and factual way, she tells about how deeper connections fed her. Analysis renewed her commitment to write, seriously, and at greater cost. It burned off layers of inhibiting denials. It rejoined her spirit to infinite energy. By writing about dreams, she shows us an old door, a heavy one, that every being rubs against. This book may help the reader to decide to push it open.

Wallis Wilde-Menozzi

By Way of Introduction

I did not set out to write this book, but when I entered a Jungian analysis, more and more people questioned me. "An analysis?" they asked. "What's wrong with you? Aren't you happy with yourself, your family, your writing?"

I said I didn't think anything was "wrong" with me, rather I was searching for something deeper. I tried to explain the dimension of an analysis which deals with soul, the pondering alone in the night and the sharing with someone.

Then, at a writers conference in New York, summer 1992, I woke early one morning with the title and chapters of this book clear in my mind. I'd call it *Looking For Gold*. Each chapter would treat a dream image from my first year of analysis – out of control, cat at the door, maple tree, green frogs, witch in the yard, vertigo… I'd write about each dream as I'd throw a pebble in the water. I'd look at the ripples as the circles widened and overlapped.

Back in Geneva, I took the idea to Keller, my analyst.[1] He said, "Go with it." So for one year, I wrote about dreams. Fiction or non-fiction? Certainly the dreams, the analysis, the life experiences were mine, making it non-fiction. But it was so much mine, how I saw and heard it, how I imagined it, that it was also fiction, in a way that Hermes, the Trickster God, might well recognize.

---

1. For obvious reasons, the analyst's name is a pseudonym.

By the time I got to the witch in my back yard, I realized my dreams were closely following the seasons. I had planted my maple tree in the fall, traveled into the dark with my frogs in the winter, experienced vertigo, and was looking forward to spring time and new life. The dreams were in harmony with the cycles of the earth.

My second year of analysis was all the richer because of this ripening of the first year. It was truly an *opus*, as in alchemy, difficult and obscure. Earlier dreams were distilled into new meanings which touched later dreams and reflections. The ever widening circles were becoming concentric.

In September 1993, I gave my manuscript to Keller. I was entering my third year of analysis, the sessions attuned to the seasons of my life and dreams. The goal of finding the darker, more soulful part of life had become the way of my analysis.

"You know," Keller said, "if you had asked your unconscious for a good story, it could not have given you a better one."

I thank all those who helped me along the way, both Keller my analyst and Pierre my husband – cellar and stone, telling images, one accompanying me downward, the other keeping me here on earth. I thank also Kim, Wallis, Kristina, Jo Ann and so many other friends.

And now I share this work with you the reader, hoping that somewhere in the stillness of the night, gold too will find you.

"For everything there is a season,
and a time for every matter under heaven…"

Ecclesiastes 3,1

1. Going Somewhere

I am going somewhere to have my shoulder healed.
There is a woman to my left and a man to my right, I do
not see their faces. We are walking down a large staircase,
the three of us abreast, descending many stairs, all the
way to the basement. Here everything is dark and obscure, we have to walk around obstacles to find a table
where I can lie down.

I ask the woman if the operation will hurt. She says my
shoulder has been put to sleep. I touch it and tell her that
it doesn't feel asleep. She says that only the surface is
awake and that underneath it is asleep.

Across the large basement room, a doctor is walking in
my direction. I recognize him as an old friend, tall and
attractive. He is dressed in a dark suit. He sits down, says
nothing, and looks at my shoulder. I feel that it will be
healed.

(March 19, 1991)

This was my dream the night before my first session
with an analyst. I am a writer, a woman writer. I am also a
wife, a mother and a grandmother, and a friend of many
wonderful people. I am fifty-eight years old and decided
two years ago that I wanted to deepen the way I was living,
the way I was writing. I had been reading a lot of Carl
Jung's thinking and felt it was time to assimilate it, to take
it down to the heart instead of leaving in the head. And in
so doing I wanted to find a way into my unconscious, to
learn to live in both worlds, the visible and the invisible.

I asked one of my friends, a Swedish Jungian analyst
who had worked in Switzerland, to suggest an analyst here

in Geneva. She sent me a list of about ten, saying I should shop around until I found one who really fit. I seriously questioned how I would know. This was all new territory to me, and I felt like a schoolchild being told to pick out her favorite teacher the first day of school. Finally I chose two from the list, a Swiss man and an English woman, both of them having trained at the Jungian Institute at Zurich. I first telephoned to the Swiss analyst, saying I wished to see him and explain my desire to start an analysis in the fall. He set a date in a month's time. Then I called the English woman. She had an opening the following week so I would go to her first.

That was that, and I went about my daily life, wondering where I had found the courage to call these two people. When Wednesday arrived, I woke up early in the morning with my shoulder numb. The entire dream came back, in playback first, image upon image. I had written it down on my computer in the middle of the night. This is the dream that is copied above. It seemed made up, invented, so many of the details obviously symbolic. I was still more anxious about the coming analysis than before.

I left home early in the afternoon to find an address which was unfamiliar to me in Geneva. Arriving ahead of time, nervous and on the defensive. I reminded myself that I had decided to do this freely and on my own, a conscious decision, an adult decision, but I still felt like the little schoolchild shopping around for the right analyst.

I also told myself that I didn't have to ever see this woman again, that maybe an analysis wasn't my thing. So many of my friends had questioned my decision. They wondered what was wrong, what I was hiding. I didn't think anything was particularly wrong with me. Physically and psychologically I felt quite well and thought I was functioning correctly. But there was another level, the soul[2] level that reaches down to the unconscious. This was the level I wanted to reach. I knew that somewhere it would communicate to the other levels.

At 3:00 exactly, Madame A. came for me and ushered me into a small study, two armchairs, a table in the middle, a bookcase along one wall, some pottery, deep yellows and browns. She was dressed similarly to me, dark skirt, light blouse, little jewelry, low heels. Her face looked familiar, a bit like that of my older sister but she was younger than I – short light brown hair, pleasant face, glasses. For a moment we looked at one another over the table.

I explained where I was in life. Marriage: French husband, met at the University of Grenoble, intercultural differences, he traveled a great deal, we had moved around Europe. Family: six children, aged 32 to 20, ranging from doctor to dancer, four married, several grandchildren, youngest son came to us from Vietnam. Work: a writer, freelancing now that the children have left home, short stories, an unpublished novel, a collection of essays with an agent, leader of a women writers workshop.

I tried to be honest, to say that all this was well and good, but perhaps a bit too good, I needed to mess it up a bit, find some dark areas, dig my heels into the dirt, maybe also my fingernails. Still everything hadn't been

2. "It is impossible to define precisely what the soul is. Definition is an intellectual enterprise anyway; the soul prefers to imagine... Soul is not a thing, but a quality or a dimension of experiencing life and ourselves." Thomas Moore, *Care of the Soul*, Harper Collins, New York, 1992, p. xi, p. 5.

"If the human soul is anything, it must be of unimaginable complexity and diversity, so that it cannot possibly be approached through a mere psychology of instinct. I can only gaze with wonder and awe at the depths and heights of our psychic nature." C.G. Jung, *Freud and Psychoanalysis*, Coll. Works, Vol. 4, p. 331 (Glossary, *Memories, Dreams, Reflections* by C.G. Jung, recorded and edited by Aniela Jaffé, Flamingo, London, 1983).

all that easy, there'd been illness, accidents, jealousy, anorexia, drugs, bouts with the police, violence, but I tended to gloss it over and make it all right. I always wanted everyone to get along, everything to go well.

Fair enough, she said. And spiritually?

I'm Catholic, I explained, converted from a Protestant background after university, after studying contemporary French writers and thinkers, and after meeting my future French husband and his family. I had a deep spiritual hunger for the Eucharist as a way to approach God and behold incarnation – God becoming man so that man becomes God[3]. After marriage, Pierre and I were active in different church movements in Europe, Pax Romana, prayer groups, weekend retreats. And when we moved to Geneva in 1970, I found quiet and solitude at the monastery of the Petites Sœurs de Bethléem on top of the Voirons mountains in nearby France. I finished my little summary saying that I saw God as a source of love, as a way of naming what Jung called the collective unconscious[4].

Madame A. smiled. She moved back to the Petites Sœurs, the little sisters of Bethlehem. She too had often

3. This indwelling of the divinity was expressed by St. Irenaeus, a Western theologian from the East, bishop of Lyons 130-200, "God became human in order that humans might become God." Matthew Fox, *Original Blessing*, Bear & Company, Santa Fe, 1983, p. 48.

4. Jung distinguished two layers of the unconscious, the personal ("unconscious contents of the individual personality") and the collective ("primordial images common to all men"). "The collective unconscious contains the whole spiritual heritage of mankind's evolution, born anew in the brain structure of every individual." C.G. Jung, *The Structure and Dynamics of the Psyche*, Coll. Works, Vol. 8, pars. 283-342 (*The Portable Jung*, edited by Joseph Campbell, Penguin Books, New York, 1987, pp. 23-46).

Jung in a 1933 seminar said, "For the collective unconscious we could use the word God... But I prefer not to use big words. I am quite satisfied with humble scientific language because it has the great advantage of bringing that whole experience into our immediate vicinity." Edward Edinger, *The Creation of Consciousness*, Inner City Books, Toronto, 1984, p. 66.

gone to their monastery above Geneva. We were speaking English. I didn't know anything else about her, other than she was married to a Swiss and had two adult children. I felt that perhaps I was discovering the fit my friend had spoken about. It was all pleasant, as if I were talking to a new acquaintance. I wanted her now to talk about herself. I was ready to sit back and ask her questions.

"Do you have a dream to work with?" she asked.

I was startled. A dream? "For this one session?" I asked.

"Yes," she replied, "this way you'll see how the dream will guide us."[5] Each week, she explained, I would bring one dream to our session The other dreams I would write down and bring to her once a month. She'd read them but we would not have time to work on more than one dream at each session.

I asked her what would happen if I stopped dreaming. I had been writing down my dreams for about two years. They were irregular. I was worried they would become still more so.

"Don't worry," she replied. "And now tell me your dream."

I related my dream, as it is written above, putting myself back into it, going down the staircase, lying on the metal table, waiting for the doctor.

"How did you feel about this dream?"

I said it had seemed very real, that my shoulder was actually aching when I woke up, that I was unable to write it all down so I went to my small computer. And when I

---

5. Since dream is our subject, here is Jung's definition: "The dream is a little hidden door in the innermost and most secret recesses of the psyche, opening into that cosmic night which was psyche long before there was any ego consciousness, and which will remain psyche no matter how far our ego consciousness may extend." C.G. Jung, *Civilization in Transition*, Coll. Works, Vol. 10 (Glossary, *Memories, Dreams, Reflections by C.G. Jung*).

returned to bed, my shoulder was still numb. But I had
felt also very uneasy, even suspicious, in writing it down. It
was just the night before our meeting, I had read about
initial dreams and their importance. Some of the details
sounded too evident, the long wide staircase, the woman
to my right and man to my left, the cellar, hints of
alchemy, experiments, the darkness, my shoulder asleep
underneath.

"And what happened to your shoulder? Why did it need
to be healed?"

My shoulder? I fell on the staircase in our house and
pulled it apart, split the rotator cuff, tore the ligaments.
Almost ten years ago. The injury slowed me down and
made me change my habits, the way I was living. I could
no longer do housework – vacuum or iron. I couldn't ski,
I couldn't play tennis, sports I did with Pierre. I had to
change my car and get an automatic gear shift. I couldn't
write by hand and even tapping the keys of my electric
typewriter tensed my arm until I changed and bought a
portable computer. I saw doctors and specialists of all
sorts, finally a surgeon in New York City. He said there was
little chance that an operation would be successful. So I
learned to live with it and I guess it was an opportunity for
me to live differently, to live more inwardly.

"What's important is the crack," she said.

Her words flustered me. There was a crack in my
shoulder. Yes. But at the same time there was another
crack. Still longer ago, I had had a car accident, coming
down from the Voirons, from the monastery which we
had talked about. I had gone there alone for a day of
prayer. I was driving back home when a bee had flown
into the car. Instead of stopping, I tried to kill it and drove
right into a cliff. I had turned over twice and pulled myself
out of the wreck, picking up the water jug I had bought at

the monastery – an earthenware jug, pottery which the sisters made, wrapped in one sheet of newspaper. An ambulance carried me to the hospital at Geneva. I was not hurt nor was the jug. The car was finished.

Then with time a crack started to appear on the jug, a fine line was etching its way onto the smooth gray surface. I wrote a story about the water jug, explaining how the crack was within, making the jug vulnerable. I had never linked the two cracks together, the one of the water jug and the one of my shoulder.

"It is through this crack in your shoulder that you will enter and go deeper. It may hurt."

I felt ready for this. I wanted to confront the dark, to feel it around me.

The time was up. She outlined the specifics of an analysis, the cost, the commitment, the scheduling. I didn't listen well. It was hard to shift gears and understand the practical things she was saying.

I walked out into the streets of Geneva, as if dazed, trying to keep my balance. I held myself still, trying to realize where I was, fearful I would not find my way home. I was mystified, intrigued, how had we come to talk about my water jug and the crack?

This had been my first good short story, the one I had taken to the workshop in New York and which served as an introduction to my blind writer professor, Robert Russell, and to a new poet friend, Amy Clampitt. They were the first people who gave me confidence in my writing.

And now this crack was going to lead me further.

I would tell my Swedish friend she had been right. I had found a fit with this first analyst in Geneva. It all seemed quite unbelievable but I had come to see – and appreciate – the unbelievable in so many things which happened.

The whole idea of synchronicity, of what Jung defined as meaningful coincidences in our daily lives, spoke to me deeply[6].

When an event occurs, when something happens to me in my daily life which is linked to an intuition I had, to a dream, to something in my psyche, I experience an emotional response. I feel very alive, warm, aglow. And as there is so often no way to account for the coincidence, either by causality or simply by chance, I am filled with wonder.

That I should have this dream about my shoulder the night before this first session, that the analyst should know about the Voirons, that we should end up talking about the crack in my shoulder and the crack in my water jug, all this had meaning for me. It was not just chance. If we stop and look at our experiences, they fit together at a certain layer. Jung called this layer, the collective unconsciousness. It is our heritage, filled with universal symbols,

6. "Synchronicity designates the parallelism of time and meaning between psychic and psychophysical [mental and physical] events... The term simply formulates the occurrence of meaningful coincidences... No reciprocal causal connection can be shown." C.G. Jung, *The Structure and Dynamics of the Psyche*, Coll. Works, Vol. 8, pars. 969-997 (*The Portable Jung*, Campbell, pp. 517-518).

"I chose this term [synchronicity] because the simultaneous occurrence of two meaningful but not causally connected events seemed to me an essential criterion. I am therefore using the general concept of synchronicity in the special sense of a coincidence in time of two or more causally unrelated events which have the same or a similar meaning." C.G. Jung, *The Structure and Dynamics of the Psyche*, Coll. Works, Vol. 8, p. 441 (Glossary, *Memories, Dreams, Reflections*).

Jean Shinoda Bolen relates the concepts of Tao and synchronicity, both based on the perception of the unity and interrelationship of all things. "In psychology, only C.G. Jung has addressed this issue, describing synchronistic events as manifestations of the acausal connecting principle that is equivalent to the Tao. He theorized that people as well as all animate and inanimate objects are linked through a collective unconscious." Bolen, *The Tao of Psychology*, Harper & Row, San Francisco, 1979, p. 6.

with archetypes[7] that we share with all peoples. When this layer is reached, there can be – in shared circumstances – synchronicity. A common chord in us vibrates.

The doctor figure in my dream, the man in the dark suit, was the husband of a very good friend. They live close to San Francisco, some 10,000 kilometers away. We don't see one another often, yet our lives have followed much of the same pattern. We both have six children, and unknowingly we both named the sixth child Daniel. When I was beginning to first read Jung, my friend sent me Welch's book *Spiritual Pilgrims*,[8] comparing the symbols of Jung and St. Teresa. It's an extraordinary book, showing how the symbols of spiritual life are universal, from Teresa's interior castle to Jung's tower at Bollingen. Now in my dream, our paths were again crossing.

As I walked along, rethinking all this, I had goose bumps, My arms were covered with shivering little bumps – the tell tale sign for me that something is happening, that there is synchronicity. Recently I had learned that Plato spoke of goose bumps as vestiges of long ago, when

7. Archetypes are universal patterns which come from the collective unconscious. Their images are present in religions, mythology, fairy tales, and emerge through one's dreams and visions.

"Whereas the personal unconscious consists for the most part of complexes [groups of feelings, thoughts, memories], the content of the collective unconscious is made up essentially of archetypes. The concept of the archetype indicates the existence of definite forms in the psyche which seem to be present always and everywhere." C.G. Jung, *The Archetypes and the Collective Unconscious*, Coll. Works, Vol. 9, pars. 87-110 (*Jung*, Campbell, p. 60).
8. "This work is about Christian individuation, the movement into the wholeness of one's personality as union with God deepens... Both Jung and Teresa were perceptive observers of human interiority. Teresa wrote about the soul – the human person in his or her relationship to God. Jung studied the psyche – the person in relationship to his or her own depths." John Welch, *Spiritual Pilgrims*, Paulist Press, New York, 1982, p. 1.

our souls were seen as birds, and when in taking care of them, we grew feathers.

I was on my way. The commitment of time and money still weighed me down, but I was coming to grips with it. Time, I would make it. I had always seemed to be able to find the extra hour when necessary. Money, I would contribute what I could, and the rest I would deem necessary for my well-being. It would be worth it. At least for one year, I would do an analysis.

I would take care of my soul and grow feathers.

The crack in the water jug opens into the dark.
(Pottery from the monastery on Montsvoirons)

2. Murky Water

I am going with a friend to visit an island. Finally my friend stays behind and I decide to go to the pier alone. I am taking a shortcut. The road narrows and turns into a steep snow-covered path. A child asks me to help her. I hold her hand. The path is crooked and difficult.

Now it descends abruptly. A man is climbing towards us. He has a small pointed beard and sharp eyes. I lose my footing and slip. Still holding the hand of the child, we fall downward along the path without hurting ourselves, then still further to the bottom which looks far away and dark and murky.

It is water. I keep holding the child and try to swim, calling out for help. I cannot get into shore. The tide is pushing us out. I keep swimming back towards the shoreline, calling and holding on to the little girl.

(March 9, 1991)

This was the dream I had before telephoning to the two analysts I had chosen from my friend's list. I wrote it down, shared it with a friend, and then went on to new dreams.

My meeting with the first analyst had gone so well that I hesitated to call the second and cancel the session. It seemed clear that I could work with the first. What would make me change my mind? My Swedish friend, who had given me their names, however urged me to wait. "You never know what may happen," she said over the telephone. "There's no reason for you to cancel."

So I kept the appointment and went, late in the afternoon, again arriving ahead of time but not finding his office. The address was right, his name was marked on a mailbox, but I couldn't find his door. I went up and down the steps, five flights, by foot, reading all the names on the doors, but there was no M. Keller.

The name alone had worried my husband. He had shown some interest when I started reading Jung and then tolerance when I started considering an analysis. But this Keller. Why the German word for cellar, for the basement? Had he chosen it to be an analyst? Couldn't he just have a normal name like the rest of us. "Like Tiberghien?" I had answered.

While back in the front hall, wondering what to do and hesitating to leave, I saw another door underneath the staircase. I read the name. Keller.

I rang once and waited. I heard someone climbing steps. The door opened. There stood the man with the pointed beard and sharp eyes – the man I had dreamed about a month earlier when I was choosing the two analysts. I had put the dream away, in my dream journal, there under my arm.

I walked down the seven steps carefully. He told me to please wait a few minutes, he was still with someone. I sat down with relief. My heart was racing. How could it be? I had never seen this analyst. No one had told me what he looked like. And yet here he was with the same pointed beard and catlike eyes.

He ushered someone else out and turned to lead me into his office, half in the basement, a small window, two large armchairs and a table in the middle. Bookshelves circled the walls, except for a large desk. Two or three ancient statues and a framed Tibetan tantra of a mandala inside a square. I avoided his eyes, asking myself if I should tell him about the dream. I felt embarrassed, ready to say, "Isn't this ridiculous? I mean it is really stupid. So maybe I should go home."

He said nothing. Silence. Finally I reached for safer ground and started to talk of our phone conversation and what were my hopes for the fall. He asked me how long I had been living in Switzerland. Almost twenty years.

"And your origins?"

My origins? I was getting sidetracked from his pointed beard. I explained how my mother's parents came from Basel and Hamburg, how my grandmother had left Basel alone at age 15, her own mother having died in childbirth. In New York City, she married a young German immigrant. Her mother's engagement ring, with two diamonds and a small sapphire had come down to me and was now going to my daughters-in-law, each stone made into an engagement ring.

On my father's side, his ancestors had left Europe much earlier, his mother's family from England, his father's from Germany. At the turn of the century, his parents had left America for the Philippines, sailing on the first boat of American teachers to Manila. They met on the ship in the middle of the Pacific and were married on the island of Leyte 800 kilometers south of Manilla, where they were among the only Americans. My father and his two brothers grew up there.

We were speaking in French. Somehow it seemed right, sort of like a full circle, through roots, to come back to Switzerland and to be speaking about ancestors in French. But I also had a momentary insight into another full circle, in my own life. When I moved to Europe as an American bride becoming a French housewife, I spoke, read, dreamed in French. I became French. Then when I started to write again, I went back to English. I spoke, read, and dreamed in English. Fleetingly I perceived that perhaps I had too readily discarded my French years. Here they were again in his office.

Keller asked how I met Pierre. I spoke of my studies at Grenoble, my first visit to Pierre's house, the night his sister had died. How our car had run off the road as we were driving him home in the middle of the night, in a blinding snowstorm. His father had come to get us and take us to their house where we would have to spend the night. Christine, his sister, my age, had died in the early evening, upstairs in her room, surrounded by family. Pierre's mother asked me if I wanted to go see her.

I had never seen a dead person. I was too frightened, too foreign, too alone. That night I wrestled with God. I lay in the guest room, listening to the footsteps go up and down the stairs, to Christine's room. The staircase was over my room, the steps went right over my head. The family was keeping watch. Why had I been so afraid?

I heard myself tell Keller in so many words that this experience had been crucial in my becoming Catholic. This encounter with God had made me aware of His presence hidden away within me, presence seeking to come to light[9]. He was there in the room, not letting me fall asleep. Like Jacob with his angel, I had fought all night with him, asking his meaning[10].

---

9. Many years later in reading Jung's *Answer to Job*, I would find confirmation of this insight. God gains in becoming conscious through His creation. "Loudly as his [Yahweh] power resounds through the universe ... it needs conscious reflection in order to exist in reality. Existence is only real when it is conscious to somebody. That is why the Creator needs conscious man..." C.G. Jung, *Answer to Job*, Viking Press, 1971, p. 535.

10. "And Jacob was left alone. And there was one that wrestled with him until daybreak, who, seeing that he could not master him, struck him in the socket of his hip, and Jacob's hip was dislocated as he wrestled with him... Jacob named the place Peniel, 'Because I have seen God face to face,' he said, 'and I have survived.'" Genesis, 32: 23-32, *The Jerusalem Bible*, Darton, Longman & Todd, London, 1974. (All biblical references are from this translation except the last, p. 172.)

Unexpectedly, I found myself once again alone in the large house of my future parents-in-law, wrestling with the angel while Pierre's family kept watch over Christine, my age, twenty-two, too young to die, the second and last daughter in a family of ten children.

I tried to get back into a date line, into chronological order. I knew the hour was passing. Where was I? I was confused. I tried to move forward to today, marriage, children, reading, writing, Jung.

"And dreams?"

Dreams. Yes. I pulled myself together and reached for my dream book. I said yes, I wished to share one with him, "a very unusual one, for I saw you in it." I paused a moment and then said, "there was a man with your face and your pointed beard."

He moved backwards, not physically, but somehow I could feel his energy body recoil ever so slightly. Not wanting to embarrass him, I kept on talking, "In my dream, I am going with a friend to visit an island..." I told the dream.

I told him also that I remembered having written about the dream in a letter to a close friend, writing that I had dreamed about someone who was climbing a path opposite me and who made me fall to the bottom of a steep hill, into dark murky water. I expressed my discomfort with this. How is this possible? It was too strange.

Keller said it was indeed unusual. All the more so for he remembered seeing quite recently a photograph of a muddy dark estuary, of what it looked like when the tide let the water out. My telling of the dream had brought back into memory the photo. Often it is this way, he said, one thing triggers another, when working with dreams. Then, leaving to the side the striking similarity of his personal appearance and that of the figure in my dream, he asked me what I recalled of the black murky water and the tides.

I replied that the water was heavy and thick and the tides kept taking me away from the shore.

As the tides in my dream were going out, he said I was going to have to swim through mud, like in an estuary.

"What does that make you think of?" he asked

"What, mud?"

"Yes, mud."

"Darkness. All the stuff I am not in touch with. I guess my shadow[11], that part of me which I've hidden away and now can't find."

What was down there in that murky water? What stuff was I going to have to swim through? I remembered another recent dream where I was taking care of a little boy and he dirtied his pants. I cleaned it all up. I washed him and dressed him again. I wanted to find the dream in my journal but there was not enough time left. I just briefly retold it, seeing again the small boy in front of me, dirtying his pants right there, full of ... shit. I smiled,

---

11. The shadow is an unconscious part of the personality with both positive and negative traits which the conscious ego tends to reject or ignore.

"For Jung, there are two kinds of shadow: one consists of the possibilities in life that we reject because of certain choices we have made... Jung also believed there is an absolute shadow, not relative to our life choices and habits. In other words there is evil in the world and in the human heart." Moore, *Care of the Soul*, p. 16.

Robert A. Johnson explores our need to "own our own shadow." He describes how it is formed through the process of acculturation and how it can wreak havoc if it is not assimilated. "To honor and accept one's own shadow is a profound spiritual discipline." Johnson, *Owning Your Own Shadow*, Harper, San Francisco, 1990, p. x.

Robert Bly speaks of eating our shadow. "If the ancients were right that darkness contains intelligence and nourishment and even information, then the person who has eaten some of his or her shadow is more energetic as well as more intelligent." Bly, *A Little Book on the Human Shadow*, Harper San Francisco, 1988, p. 42.

realizing how hard it was for me to say this word. I could see the boy all clean again, but I couldn't see the ... shit.

It was time to leave. I asked M. Keller about the conditions. I wanted to ask again what would happen if I discovered there was nothing down there in the murky water. What would happen if I learned I was empty inside? Instead I looked up and saw the short pointed beard of the man in my dream. I saw the same yellow cat's eyes, daring me to look in the dark.

Instead I heard myself say that I wished to start the analysis in September. I knew the choice of analyst had been made for me. My dream had led me there, to this room seven steps down in the underground.

As I stumbled out into the daylight, I tried saying shit. Shit, shit, shit. Why was it so difficult? I saw an image of myself which I didn't like: little Miss Goodie, fussing to make everything clean and nice. I had been well trained. How many diapers had I changed and washed for six children. I could still see them, yellow stained – for I had nursed those babies – hanging all over the bathroom. And going one step further I saw most of my writing as clean and nice. Maybe there were some stains but the pages had all been washed.

I remembered when my son Christopher, the pianist-composer, asked me if any of my stories were entitled, "It's all right." I heard his question and laughed, recognizing the truth in it. So many of my stories could be entitled "It's all right." I would take an experience that was difficult, frighteningly difficult, I would hint at it, and then I would make it all right. Daniel's story, for example, his arrival at the airport in Geneva, all of us waiting, waiting for months, for the last plane out of Saigon before the Viet Cong closed the airport.

Daniel arrives, two years old, terrorized. Pierre at the gate stands him up for us to see. Daniel falls down. He cannot stand up alone. He falls down on the floor and hits his head against the tile floor. Then he hits it again, hard against the floor, and again. When I wrote the story, I took out the last line.

By camouflaging the truth, by hiding his anger, it was taking me a longer time to understand it, to come to grips with it. It was also taking Daniel a longer time to come to grips with something his mother was denying. And it was perhaps encouraging the reader to see only the lightness of Daniel's arrival. Five brothers and sisters, a mother and father, all waiting to hold him in their arms. Where was the darkness, the child who didn't want to leave his country and never asked to come to us, who found the tile floor of the Geneva airport so cold and so unyielding?

Is this peculiar to the woman writer? How many of us conceal, consciously or unconsciously, our pain, our suffering, our despair? How many of us write about the joy of childbirth without writing about its agony, the terrifying rupture, when the mother feels her womb is being ripped open, when she affronts what she thinks is her wrenching death? And then the final eruption. Virginia Woolf remarked that "very few women yet have written truthful autobiographies."[12] From Plath, Sexton, Rich, and Woolf, we learn about what happens when women explore their previously hidden resentments and experiences, guilts and sufferings.

12. Carolyn Heilbrun reveals how women throughout centuries have suppressed the truth of their own experiences in order to conform to what is expected of them by the patriarchal society they are living in. "There will be narratives of female lives only when women no longer live their lives isolated in the houses and the stories of men." Heilbrun *Writing a Woman's Life*, Ballantine Books, New York, 1988, p. 47.

Heilbrun looks forward to when women, born into the women's movement and escaping the usual rhythms of the traditional female existence, discover the freedom and courage to take risks, to be courageous, to write their own story. "She may well for the first time be woman herself." p. 131.

Certainly I had gained in living in the house of my husband, in acquiring another language, another culture, in having so many children. But what had I lost in giving up my own house, my language, my culture? What had I felt in all the years of bringing up children, in diapering babies, waking to their cries and fevers in the middle of the night, watching them grow, tending their tempers, their distress, their unending demands?

"What would happen," wrote Muriel Rukeyser, "if one woman told the truth about her life? The world would split open."

The world would split open.

Was I ready? I wanted to try.

3. Out of Control

I am driving a poet friend from New York down the hill at Grand Saconnex towards Geneva. She is telling me my car is not working, but I am talking about something else and not listening to her. I am certain it's working because it recently broke down and a car doesn't break down twice in a row.
Then I realize it is not working. I cannot brake. I can hardly steer and I have a lot of speed. I manage to veer off the road and drive into an open space where I circle up a hill, slowly losing speed until stopping right on the very top.
The poet friend is no longer there. Instead there is a black dog who wants to get down from the hill. I call to two men to come help because it is dangerous to leave the car on such a high hilltop. As I tell the men my story, the dog runs off. More men come to help. They will come carry the car to a safer place where I can leave it.
(September 29, 1991)

I was anxious about this dream. It was September, I had just started my analysis, and I thought the dream was pessimistic. It was disheartening, discouraging. Here I was, the I figure in the dream, driving to Geneva with a poet friend whom I recognized as a workshop director and a good poet from New York, one whom I had met that summer.

Instead of listening to her and driving more carefully, I was paying no attention and speeding. The only way to stop the car was to go off the road and drive up a hill until the car slowed down on its own and stopped at the very top. All this because I was not listening to my poet friend, my muse. That is how I saw the dream, and I was angry with myself.

How could I get anywhere with my writing and with my analysis if I continued to go too fast and didn't pay attention? This was the question I would ask Keller.

I was going once a week, each Wednesday afternoon. I almost always brought a dream, along with some experience of the week and some idea of what I was writing. I'd start the session with a short description of what I was living, reading, writing. Keller would listen, nod, look at me, stretch, maybe yawn, and sometimes hint at something, give an example. We'd talk about it. Then I'd try to choose a dream. When I had asked him how to choose – for in the beginning of my analysis I was flooded with dreams – he said to let the dream choose me.

So I let the above dream choose me and related it, feeling again the speed and lack of direction, sharing it in French. This was not difficult, when a word escaped me, I'd say it in English. Language did not bother me. I soon understood that analysts work in many languages, for deep down the language of the unconscious, the language of dreams, is universal.

I told Keller that I did not like the dream. Why had I not listened to my poet friend from New York? I would then not have had the accident.

"What would have happened," he asked, "if you had not lost control of the car?"

I hadn't thought in that direction. "I guess I would have gone to Geneva with my poet friend."

"And that would have been very nice, a very nice thing for two writers to do, to go to Geneva for a cup of tea." Keller's voice was sing-song. "But there would have been no story. No hilltop, no dog running away, no men. No speed, no story." He paused, then repeated strongly, for emphasis, "No speed, no story."

There was silence.

"But what about my friend in the car who told me to drive more slowly?" I asked. "She is a poet whose work I like, a muse?"

"A poet in a dream is not necessarily a muse, even if you like her work. She can also be an alter ego, another ego voice, telling you to watch the car, drive slowly, stay on the main road, be careful, and above all don't lose control."

The texture of the dream images shifted. His suggestion of a nice quiet cup of tea – warm and cozy – in downtown Geneva was indeed less exciting than circling to the top of a hill.

He asked me if I had seen a recent prize-winning movie, *La Belle Noiseuse*, about a famous French painter, Frenhofer, who had been unable to finish a last painting and couldn't get beyond arranging his paints and his brushes. Before he could create a new work of art, he had to first let go, let go of his control, of his old sketches and models. The artist can not follow a road and a speed limit – a set of rules – to create. Somewhere along the way, he has to go off the road. He has to break the rules and free his inspiration.

I was nodding my head. The night before I had pulled up on my computer screen an old story, thinking to rewrite it and submit it to an anthology in the States. It was called "Tinker, Tailor." I liked the title. The piece was about a woman's life, her choice of schooling and profession. Would she be a tinker or a tailor? It was about my life, what I had wanted to be when I was in school, and how my choice of a profession: violinist or professor, changed as I left school to my choice of a role: wife and mother.

When I started to rework the essay, there was a long part in the middle about the perfect wife in the Book of Proverbs, the wife who stays up all night, mending and cooking. "A perfect wife, who can find her? She is far beyond the price of pearls... She keeps good watch on the conduct of her household, no bread of idleness for her." (Proverbs 31, 10-31) As I reread it, I was terribly bored by the entire passage so I took it out. I pushed a couple of buttons on my computer and deleted it. The piece seemed tighter, certainly shorter.

Slowly I took more and more chunks out of the story. Finally I broke it all to pieces and deleted every single word and letter from the screen. Nothing was left. I went to bed exhilarated, and with a feeling of freedom.

"That's it," said Keller when I told him why I was nodding, what I had done to my old story. "Like in the movie, you let go of the old model. Something new will emerge. If you had held on to the old piece, you would have driven down to Geneva and had your cup of tea."

So in my dream, my unconscious was telling me to move ahead. Go on, take risks, forget about control. But if one of my old stories still works, I was asking myself, then what? How many old models do I have to break?

"This doesn't mean you have to get rid of all your old stories," said Keller, anticipating my question. "It just means that too much control stifles creativity. There has to be a crack, an opening somewhere for the unconscious."

A crack, somewhere...

I was jolted back into the crack in my water jug, to my car accident when I was coming down the mountainside, after visiting the monastery. I had talked about this accident to the woman analyst, but not to Keller.

Yes, I had lost control. The car crashed into the cliff and I lost consciousness. Keller had said "There has to be an opening somewhere for the unconscious."

After the accident, back home, the jug looked whole but there was a crack inside it. I looked whole, but there was a crack inside me also. I had become vulnerable. And this was my first good piece of writing, my first story. "No speed, no story," he had said.

I started to explain this to Keller, but time was running out. He didn't move, but I slowed up. My earthenware water jug was more numinous than ever. I could see the crack, I could see the jug resting on the mantle above the fireplace in our living room. I could see it telling the story of why I was now in Keller' office – letting in both light and darkness – there in his half-basement, seven steps down from the front hall.

I went home, remembering something I had read about living symbols and locating images in our lives and dreams. It was in the book my friend in California had sent me, comparing the spiritual path of Jung and that of Teresa of Avila. I found the passage, "The telling of our story requires that we image our experience. The images may become symbols which point to the sacred levels in our lives where God contacts us and calls us to life."[13]

13. The text continues, "These predominant images will give unity and flow to other images in our lives, sub-symbols relating to our experience. Often these images have been with us a long time, but we have never reflected upon them or allowed them to speak to us." Welch, *Spiritual Pilgrims*, p. 55.

Julia Jewett in an incisive essay, "Womansoul," wrote, "Jung has observed that the person who has the living symbol is the one who will be able to make the journey. There has to be a strengthening connection, in order for the individual not to stand alone." *Jung's Challenge to Contemporary Religion*, edited by Murray Stein and Robert Moore, Chiron Publications, Illinois, 1987, p. 164.

Marie Louise von Franz pointed out the cyclical process in the creation of a symbol, "You might say that the unconscious produces a symbol, and that the conscious is inspired by it, reproduces it, forms it, and gives it expression, which in turn influences the unconscious." von Franz, *Shadow and Evil in Fairy Tales*, Spring Publications, Dallas, 1974, p. 79.

The ancient stone well speaks of living water.
(Isle of Port Cros, France)

Author John Welch suggested that we begin our story by finding a predominant image, one which powerfully affects us and leads us deeper.

So be it. I had found my image – the water jug – or it had found me. It spoke to me of roundness, of circles of clay, of stone wells, fountains, water. It spoke of the living water that Jesus offered to the Samaritan woman at Jacob's well. "The water that I shall give will turn into a spring, a spring of water welling up to eternal life."[14] This spring of water was within me. I had only to let it flow.

My water jug spoke to me also of the grail, the chalice of the Mass, symbolizing our spiritual goal, union with the divine. The legends of the Holy Grail relate the quest for this vessel of inner wholeness – ourselves and our Creator, the conscious and the unconscious, and also the masculine and the feminine. As Emma Jung, edited by Marie-Louise von Franz, wrote in her profound study on the Grail, each human being represents a place of transformation, a vessel in which the opposites meet together.[15]

The story begins with Joseph of Arimathaea who is believed to have brought the original cup, used by Christ at the Last Supper, to the western world. By the age of King Arthur, in the 1100's, the medieval stage is set for the quest. The knights of the Round Table pledge themselves to go in search of the mysterious Grail.

14. John, 4: 14. This promise of living water is repeated in John 7: 37-38, "If any man is thirsty, let him come to me. As the scripture says, From his breast shall flow fountains of living water."
    Water contains a sense of eternity. He who drinks of this living water, participates already in eternal life. *Dictionnaire des Symboles,* Jean Chevalier, Alain Gheerbrant, Editions Robert Laffont / Jupiter, Paris 1982, p. 377.
15. "For this task [reconciliation of opposites] the individual human being serves as a *vessel,* for only when the opposites are reconciled in the single individual can they be united. The individual therefore becomes a receptacle ... a place of transformation and a *vessel* in which God may come to consciousness." Emma Jung, edited by M.L. von Franz, *The Grail Legend,* Sigo Press, Boston, 1986, p. 90.

In the legend we are most familiar with, it is Parsifal who ventures into the Grail castle and sees the wounded Fisher King. The Grail is in the castle but it is only when Parsifal asks the King what is wrong that the Grail is able to heal. It is only when we see our imperfections – the crack in the jug – that we can ask the right question.

In *The Heroines Journey*, Maureen Murdock writes that in our culture, we are like the Fisher King in our wounding. We do not recognize the Grail within us. Our unrelated masculine nature, demanding perfection and control, refuses to listen to our intuition and feelings. "The Grail is the symbol of the sacred, creative feminine principle which is accessible to all of us. The Grail can heal the King just as the feminine can heal our masculine nature."[16] But we must open our eyes to the suffering, to the darker side.

My water jug was there to heal me, to remind me that I have only to let love flow through me, keeping me aware and creative. I didn't have to follow any rules or strive for control. The crack on my jug showed me the way. It was through it that I could bring the light of consciousness into the darkness, into my darker feminine side.

During the weeks and months that followed, I tried to forget about control and perfection, about rules and roles and straight roads. But it was not easy. There was resistance. There was my poet friend, my alter ego, sitting in the car, telling me I was going too fast, that the car wasn't working, that I would never succeed. There were the

16. "The masculine is an archetypal force, it is not a gender. Like the feminine, it is a creative force that lives within all women and men. When it becomes unbalanced and unrelated to life, it becomes combative, critical, and destructive." Murdock, *Heroine's Journey*, Shambhala, Boston, 1990, p. 156.
    The healing occurs through the unity of opposites, the unity of the masculine and the feminine. In the legend, the masculine is embodied in the King, the feminine in the Grail. The wasteland flowers when they are brought together.

women in the writers workshop, which I've been leading for over eight years, with long established habits.

There was my husband, my family, the "Mom, are you there?" There was the parish council and the leadership roles in the church. There was my ego, my conscious mediator, all the years of forging ahead, of achieving, of being in the top of the class. Only through relating to the unconscious, could I learn to go into unchartered lands and discover new life, new creativity, uniting the masculine and the feminine. "Soul enters life from below," wrote Thomas Moore, "through the cracks, finding an opening into life at the points where smooth functioning breaks down."[17]

Like in my dream, I kept thinking my car – my organized ego – was working, for in my mind accidents don't happen twice in a row. But they happen day after day if we let them. And they happen even in the same dream, for dreams are never over, they have no beginning, no end. They are like evocative paintings, gifts from our unconscious, paintings which deepen each time we look at them.

I enter once again into my dream. I lose control and climb to the top of the hill. I can not stay there, I call for help, for strong masculine arms to get me down to safer ground. And this time as I relive my dream, I remember trying to hold on to the small black dog. He was inside the car. I wanted him to stay there, safe from danger.

I was still reining in my instinctual side. My poet friend was gone, but the black dog was there. He was young and playful. I wanted to keep him with me. But instead, he ran

17. The author here is speaking of the family as crucible. "But care of the soul doesn't require fixing the family or becoming free of it. We may need simply to recover soul by reflecting deeply on the soul events that have taken place in the crucible of the family." Moore, *Care of the Soul*, pp. 26-27.

off and down the hill, showing me the way from the visible world to the invisible. If I had not picked up speed and veered off the road, without brakes, the dog would have stayed inside the car, locked in my conscious self – so locked in that I was not even aware he was there.

"No speed, no story," said Keller.

"No crack, no healing," said my water jug.

4. Cat at the Door

I am sleeping in a very large, old-fashioned apartment on the ground floor of a turn of the century building. It is our apartment but Pierre and the children are not there. I arrived the night before, entering with a woman friend from the back courtyard.

In the morning we are up and getting ready to leave. I am standing in the front hall of the apartment when suddenly the door opens against me and a black cat comes in on its own. I am very surprised and look outside to see who let it in. There is no one, just the empty front hall of the apartment building.

I close the door and go to tell my friend what happened.

(November 20, 1991)

The apartment could have been our apartment in Brussels, on the ground floor of an old stone building. We lived there during the early years of our marriage. There was a small back courtyard with a circular path where the children played. My desk, in our bedroom, faced one of the French windows which opened out into the yard. I used to write there every free moment. We didn't have any cats.

Later, much later, when we lived in an ancient priory in France, we acquired our first cat, a tabby, striped beige and black. She is still with us, has outlasted our children here in our house in Switzerland, and diverts us from time to time by playing the piano, hopping onto the keys and strolling up and down.

The cat in my dream was black, all black. When it entered the apartment, it went straight past me, as if it knew the way. I remember being very startled. I had never seen this black cat before. And the door had opened on its own, there was no one on the other side. The wide front hall was absolutely empty.

I told Keller about the dream at the end of our weekly session. I had been expressing anxiety about my analysis, or rather about my inner life, worrying that it might be rather unimaginative, even empty, empty because there might be nothing there.

He asked me how I felt about the cat. Was it intruding? Or was it welcome?

I said it had surprised me, but that it was welcome and it was friendly. It had entered as if it knew its way.

Keller suggested that the dream seemed to answer my anxieties. At the door in my dream, at the door to my unconscious, there was indeed something. There was a cat. I did not have to fear there was nothing, instead there was the unexpected, the irrational, the instinctual. So it is, when the unconscious wakes us, it comes like a thief in the middle of the night. We cannot plan for its visit. We have only to wait. We cannot make the cat come, we can not direct the cat, it comes when it wants, it comes on its own. But we must be waiting.

We spoke of the five wise bridesmaids and the five foolish bridesmaids of the Gospel. When the bridegroom arrived at midnight, the foolish ones had left to buy oil for their lamps, and when they returned, the door to the wedding hall was closed. They cry to the lord, open the door. He replies that he does not know them. And the door remains closed. "So stay awake," ends the story, "because you do not know either the day or the hour." (Matthew 25, 1-14)

My dream was counseling me to stay awake. I do not know when the cat will appear at the door. I have only to remain watchful, ready to let it in. Watchful for the unforeseen, for the unexpected.

Marie Louis von Franz, C.G. Jung's close associate in Zurich, described the cat as a figure of the anima[18], of our creative and imaginative side. In the fairy tale, "The Frog-Daughter of the Tsar," the cat appears when the beautiful princess creates a magical garden. In the middle of the garden there is a cat dancing around a column. It climbs to the top and sings folk songs. When it comes back down, it recites fairy tales. The young princess and all the guests at the ball watch the cat in delight and wonder, like little children.[19]

In her interpretation of this tale, von Franz wrote that the cat refers to the close relationship between the anima and man's capacity to create art and to enter into the world of imagination. The imaginary is not an illusion. It wells up from the depths of man's being and creates a

18. In Jungian terminology, the anima (Latin, "soul") is the unconscious, feminine side of a man's personality; the animus (Latin, "spirit") is the unconscious, masculine side of a woman's personality.

"Just as man is compensated by a feminine element, so woman is compensated by a masculine element... This results in a considerable psychological difference between men and women... The animus corresponds to the paternal Logos just as the anima corresponds to the maternal Eros." C.G. Jung, *Aion*, Coll. Works, Vol. 9/II, pars. 1-42 (*Jung*, Campbell, pp. 151-152).

Also see C.G. Jung, *The Visions Seminars*, Spring, Zurich, 1976, where Jung explains how the animus and the anima should function as a bridge or a door leading to the images of the collective unconscious.

John Welch wrote, "Every man has a feminine quality within him and every woman has a masculine quality within her ... When either the anima or animus is dominant in the conscious personality, the opposite pole acts as an inner personality." Welch, *Spiritual Pilgrims*, p. 165.
19. The fairy tale, "The Frog-Daughter of the Tsar" is a Russian version of the Grimms' fairy tale, "The Three Feathers." Von Franz gives a detailed psychological interpretation of this fairy tale in *Interpretation of Fairy Tales*, Spring Publications, New York City, 1970, p. 73.

symbolic world, a magical garden. A rational viewpoint
cannot understand this reality and works to destroy it, or
at least to deny it.

And so I was brought to understand that my anxieties
were too rational, that they represented that part of me
which wanted to understand, to direct, to control. If I
were to deepen my way of living and writing, it was exactly
this rational discipline that I must leave at the door. I
cannot rationally explain, nor understand, my unconscious. "The unconscious is truly unconscious," insisted
Jung[20]. Nor can I force my creativity. I can only let it open
the door on its own, like the cat in my dream.

I knew I was one of those women who could be defined
as "daughters of their fathers." We have been geared to
achievement, to success. Marion Woodman in several of
her books writes about Daddy's little girl who chooses
always to please. "Working so hard to create our own
perfection we forget we are human beings."[21] Early in life
I had identified with the values of "my father," of the male
world around me. The women were at home, the men
were at work. Their world was the world that challenged
me. I grew up thinking it was necessary to be first, first in
class, first in sports, first in music. I worked very hard, all
through high school, all through college and graduate
school.

Then I worked hard through marriage, making it dou-
bly difficult by marrying someone of another country,

20. I heard C.G. Jung say this in a video on his life and work, with his
slow insistence on each word. Then I found a reference to the written
quotation "The unconscious is unconscious and therefore can neither
be grasped nor conceived." *Mysterium Coniunctionis,* Coll. Works,
Vol. 14, p. 177.
21. Many of Marion Woodman's books, each one as excellent as the
other, are published by Inner City Books, Toronto. The quotation
comes from *Addiction to Perfection*, Inner City Books, Toronto, 1982,
p. 10.

language, religion and culture. And I continued, following him to his country and on to still other countries, having a new child with each successive move around Europe, with each new culture and language. I was still striving for A's on my report card.

Now I was being told to sit back and wait. I'd gone as far as I could. I needed now to await the unexpected, the magical garden, the cat singing folk songs, reciting fairy tales.

Some time later, I was sitting at my desk, reading through my dream journal, re-imagining some of my dreams, replaying them, listening to them anew. I was up in my small office, once the bedroom of our youngest son, Daniel. It was there that he had cried every night, with nightmares after leaving Vietnam at two years old. And every night I had cradled him in my arms, trying to push away his fears and anguish. Now he lives downtown with a friend in Geneva. The room has become my space, the walls are quiet, the windows look out into the trees.

The bell rang at the front door. We have an old bronze bell to the left of the door, with a little chain attached to the gong. I was surprised by the loud clear ring in the middle of a quiet afternoon. I went downstairs and opened the door. There was no one. Only the cat, our tabby cat, waiting to come inside. She walked straight past me. I went out onto the driveway, still no one. It seemed strange. I circled the house. There was no one. I looked around the inside of the house. Still no one.

I went back upstairs and sat down again at my desk. My eyes returned to my dream book, I turned to the next page. It was my dream of the cat, the cat at the door. It read, "the front door suddenly opened and a cat came in on its own." The coincidence was uncanny, it felt mysterious. I had been thinking about my dreams, the bell rang, there was the cat.

It was evident that the cat couldn't ring our doorbell. Then what? I went back in my notes, to what Keller had said upon the first reading of my dream. The cat was sent there to announce the arrival of someone. Keller had said it was like John the Baptist, who was sent to announce someone greater than himself. "The one who follows me is more powerful than I am, and I am not fit to carry his sandals." (Matthew 3:11) The synchronicity of it all reinforced my awareness of something other, of something stirring in my unconscious.

A few days later when I mentioned this to Keller, in the midst of other experiences and dreams, I saw him nod and doze off. I wondered if he were suddenly exhausted or was he not interested in my cat. I did not need to ask, for instead he suddenly became very awake, saying he had felt a descent, a heaviness, come upon him – as if he could have fallen asleep – as soon as I mentioned the cat. He explained that he often felt very strongly the moods and attitudes of his analysands. Here the transference[22] had been very strong. As soon as I had started to talk about the cat, he had felt my descent into the unconscious.

"Let yourself be," he said, speaking quite firmly. "You are heading towards a different creativity, perhaps not only in your writing, but also in your spiritual life. Just don't force it. Let it come on its own."

Soon afterwards, I was napping in the afternoon when I dreamed that our cat was coming in the window by my desk. In my dream the cat was very large, all round, sleepy,

22. The terms transference and countertransference describe the unconscious emotional bonds that arise through projection between two persons in an analytic relationship.
"In addition to the transference distortions of the analyst by the patient, there were also distortions of the patient by the analyst – the so called countertransference... Jung shows that the analyst and analysand are jointly involved in a process that cannot be entirely conscious and may be transformative of both partners." James Hall, *Jungian Dream Interpretation*, Inner City Books, Toronto, 1983, p. 54.

caramel in color. As it approached, it grew larger like a human figure, rounded, still caramel colored. Slowly it came to the end of the bed and crawled under the side where I was resting. I felt that it wanted to be near me and rest. I woke up unafraid, not even surprised. Instead it felt natural to have this cat-like figure lying under my bed.

At the following session, I told Keller that still another cat had come to call. He seemed to think that this visit of the caramel colored cat was to be expected. And it was quite natural that it go under my bed.

He asked if I was familiar with active imagination.

I said I'd read about it, but had never consciously tried to do it. I said that it seemed similar to dreaming, to letting images of the unconscious flow through the mind.

"Images of the unconscious, yes, but you are not dreaming. You are fully awake. You are active, not passive. Your conscious ego is participating."

He suggested that I try, that I actively re-imagine the cat figure and enter into an imaginary dialogue. "Sometime during the days ahead, when you are resting in your room, visualize the figure under your bed and try to talk with it." He said I should try to listen to it, without any preconceived ideas, without forcing any answers.

I wanted to try. There was some meaning to all these cats in my life, including our own piano playing tabby who rings the front door bell. So the next day I lay down to rest and waited until I could feel that the cat figure was there under my bed. It was lying on its side like I was. I stopped thinking and waited. The phone rang. It was Pierre. He wanted to know how I was. I said fine.

I tried again. I was quiet and listened. The phone rang again. This time it was Daniel. "Mom, I just wanted to know how you are." It was spooky. Normally Daniel doesn't call in the mid-afternoon.

This was not an auspicious beginning. I decided to try once more. I took the receiver off the phone. As I lay back on my side, it seemed the figure under my bed lay back on its side. "What do you want?" I said.

There was silence.

"What do you want?" I repeated. I waited a long time, trying to keep my mind empty.

Then I heard it say, "I just want to stay here."

So the cat and I stayed there, resting together.

I went back to what Jung had written about active imagination. He called it conscious daydreaming. First we empty our mind of mindful thinking, then through imagining – which can take the form of listening, of writing, painting, dancing – we give an outer expression to an inner image or series of images.[23]

I had experienced this in writing, when instead of willfully forcing a story out and onto paper, the story comes out on its own. Author Brenda Ueland called this creative process moodling. "The imagination needs moodling – long, inefficient, happy idling, dawdling and puttering. These people who are always briskly doing something and as busy as waltzing mice, they have little sharp, staccato ideas. But they have no slow, big ideas."[24]

23. "After the separation from Freud in 1912, Jung began his profound experiment on and in himself. The primary technique he used appears to have been active imagination, which is the name of the technique used for exploring the unconscious mind. In the simplest possible terms, active imagination is akin to conscious daydreaming." Peter O'Connor, *Understanding Jung, Understanding Yourself*, Paulist Press, New York, 1985, p. 76.

M.L. von Franz wrote of active imagination, "through which one can literally attract the contents of the unconscious. If you succeed in producing – either by drawing, or conversation, or imagination – the right kind of symbol, you can, to a certain extent, constellate your own unconscious. The achievement of the connection between conscious and unconscious is a relatively slow process." von Franz, *Shadow and Evil in Fairy Tales*, p. 74.

24. Ueland, *If You Want to Write*, Graywolf Press, Saint Paul, 1987, p.32. It is at times of "creative idleness", Ueland wrote, that we are being filled "with warm imagination." p. 34.

It was the same thing. Moodling. Active imagination. We have to be idle and alone – without phone calls from family and friends – quietly looking and daydreaming, not willing all the time. This quiet looking and moodling awakens our imagination and lets in ideas and feelings which we never guessed were inside of us.

I began turning my short "cat-naps" – how beautiful that word, now suddenly illuminated with new meaning – into wakeful daydreaming. It became very natural. I had only to lie quietly on my bed, during the day, draw the white curtains and let my mind be still.

I summon my cat-figure. I know it is there, it told me it wanted to stay. And I listen. I have to remain quiet, without interruption. I can not be rushed. When I am ready, the cat will be ready.

With time, I will enter into that magical garden. My cat – the figure of my imaginative self – will teach me to dance, to sing folk songs and recite fairy tales. And I will sit back in delight and wonder.

5. Maple Tree

It is autumn. I am walking through the woods, near a pond, with a woman writer friend. The countryside is lovely, rays of sunlight play on the yellow leaves. I walk to an open space near the pond and decide to plant a tree. I pick up a small maple tree in my arms, there are still bright yellow leaves on the branches. It is about two meters high. The roots hang down free and unattached. I put it in the humid ground, the roots go in easily, without effort.

I ask my friend if she doesn't want to plant a tree. She agrees. I tell her to take a different tree and to plant it the same way. I say that when we return to the pond next year, the open space will be filled.

(November 20, 1991)

This dream followed the dream about the cat at the door, the same night, one after the other. At first I thought more about the unexpected appearance of the black cat. But slowly the image of the small maple tree found its importance.

The dream spoke to me of my writing and of my friends in the women's writers workshop which I have been leading here in Geneva for eight years. The writer figure in the dream is a woman my age who has written all her life and who was a member of the workshop for years before I entered.

I started writing full-time only when our older children were leaving home. Then for my fiftieth birthday, I went to a workshop in New York and came back enthusiastic. I began to freelance and shortly afterwards was asked to lead the workshop in Geneva. Three years ago we brought out our first collection of stories and poems, entitled *Offshoots*, and last year we followed with *Offshoots*, Volume II, keeping the same title, a metaphor for the writing of women living in a foreign country.

My dream occurred the night after an evening of readings from our new volume. Both the writer friend of my dream and I had read. Only afterwards did I think about the timing of the dream. The night we presented *Offshoots*, the literary endeavors of women who have been uprooted and replanted in unfamiliar soil, I dreamed of planting a young tree. On the cover of the review is a black and white photo of the plane trees that border the lake in Geneva. The branches have been cut back, and new offshoots are poking out, promising new growth.

With this awareness of the dream's synchronicity, I saw it suggesting that our workshop could now look forward to a winter of quiet and of deepening. We have replanted our collection, near the water, in an open space, and next year, the space will be filled by our new work.

And I saw it suggesting the same gestation for my own writing and for my analysis. Ahead of me was winter. Thomas Merton, the Trappist monk, whose books on contemplation helped me learn to be still and silent many years ago, wrote, "O silence, golden zero / Unsetting sun / Love winter when the plant says nothing."[25]

As I lived the weeks and months after my dream, I held on to my tree. It felt good. When I was a child I had a favorite large tree. I now want to think it was a maple tree.

25. *Selected Poems of Thomas Merton*, Introduction by Mark van Duren, New Directions Books, New York City, 1967, p. 112. Merton wrote to Mark Van Duren in 1954 that poetry at its best is contemplation – of things and what they signify. "The earliest fathers, knew that all things are symbolic by their very being and nature, and all talk of something beyond themselves." p. xiiii.

I would climb in its branches, up to the top. I built a tree house, a simple platform, but it was my house. I used to sit there and dream. It was also my hiding place where I would go when I was unhappy and wanted to be alone.

My son who teaches piano and composes, now married and with one child, also has his tree, at the end of the little road opposite our house here in Geneva. There are a few fields and in the middle of one stands an ordinary tree, like many others. But only his tree is in the center. When Chris comes back for the weekend or for vacation, he often disappears for awhile. I know he is visiting his tree.

I like the idea of visiting and conversing with trees. In the myth about young Narcissus, once he has discovered the image of his inner self, he longs to be united with it. And he talks to the trees, saying, "Has anyone ever had as much longing as I have?" Thomas Moore, in *Care of the Soul*, writes of Narcissus' growing awareness. "Talking to nature shows that his grief is giving him a new connection to the soul. When soul is present, nature is alive."[26] And Moore goes on to suggest that a certain amount of talking to trees would make us less rigid in our monotheism.

Monotheism, polytheism, pantheism. As a child, I was happy to see God in everything around me. I remember reading Edna St. Vincent Millet's poem, "Renaissance," and lying down on the ground, alone in the fields near our house, looking up at the sky, imagining the blue dome coming down upon me, "and lo! Infinity came down and settled over me," and being reborn. Often I lay down in the wild high grass and stared at the sky until it

---

26. Thomas Moore, *Care of the Soul*, p. 61. In this chapter on self-love and its myth, the author wrote that true self love "is not ego loving ego, but ego loving the soul." p. 63. When Narcissus discovers the face in the pool is his own, he is given a new image of self, which engenders a sense of union with all nature.

came down upon me. When I stood up afterwards, my arms tingled, my head was dizzy, and my heart felt high. But then I was taught that polytheism and pantheism were pagan and primitive. I saw adults frowning upon communing with nature. We – whoever that was in my ten year old mind – were more advanced, we were modern thinkers, we knew better than to believe in "trees."

So I corrected myself. I decided it was not right to see God in a tree, to smell God in a rose bush. And rationally I started to work out a system of belief for myself[27], stemming from my parents' questioning faith and the Congregational church to which we belonged. As I grew older, I included some of the supports and rituals from the Episcopalian church of my prep school years. At college, I read and studied much contemporary writing and thinking. T.S. Eliot hovered over me, his prayers in *Ash Wednesday*, "Teach us to sit still / Even among these rocks, / Our peace in His will."[28]

Slowly I turned to the Catholic church, where God and creation could be one. I read Teilhard de Chardin when we were living in Brussels and when I was busy with young

27. Jung would call this system of beliefs not a religion but a creed, "whereas the meaning and purpose of religion lie in the relationship of the individual to God…" C.G. Jung, *The Undiscovered Self*, Little, Brown and Company, Boston, 1957, p. 21.

"Religion appears to me to be a peculiar attitude of mind which could be formulated in accordance with the original use of the word *religio*, meaning a careful consideration of certain dynamic factors that are conceived as 'powers.' C.G. Jung, Coll. Works 11, p. 8 (Welch, *Spiritual Pilgrims*, p. 79).

In the same light, during a 1961 televised interview on the BBC, Jung, when questioned if he believed in God, answered, "I don't need to believe, I know."

28. Eliot continued, "And even among these rocks / Sister, mother, / And spirit of the river, spirit of the sea, / Suffer me not to be separated / And let my cry come unto Thee." *American Poetry, Modern British Poetry*, edited by Louis Untermeyer, Harcourt, Brace & Company, New York, 1950, p. 421.

children, nursing the second and then the third baby. "Son of earth, steep yourself in the sea of matter, bathe in its fiery water, for it is the source of your life and your youthfulness."[29] I steeped myself in family which grounded me there where I was living in Belgium, Italy, France and then Switzerland.

Now thirty years later, I was hugging my little maple tree, carrying it to the open space near the pond. I was once again seeing the Creator in His or Her creation. No longer was God somewhere else. God was within – within me, within my tree. Matthew Fox, author of *Original Blessing*, calls this way of seeing the world, pan-en-theism: "God is in everything, everything is in God."[30]

I took my tree with me to Keller, along with my black cat, and still more dreams of leaving places.

Keller looked at me out of the corner of his eye and waited. The air between us crackled as if charged with electricity. I remembered Kim, my Swedish analyst friend,

---

29. This quotation is taken from Teilhard de Chardin's *Hymn of the Universe*, (Harper & Row, New York, 1965, p. 63) in the passage entitled The Spiritual Power of Matter. The Jesuit scholar here reveals his extraordinary experience, when walking in the desert he is overcome by his Creator. Falling to his knees he speaks the Hymn to Matter, "I acclaim you as the divine milieu, charged with creative power, as the ocean stirred by the Spirit, as the clay molded and infused with life by the incarnate Word." p. 70.
30. Matthew Fox, *Original Blessing*, p. 90. The Dominican scholar counters the fall-redemption teaching of the church ("The soul makes war with the body," Augustine) and proposes instead the creation-centered teaching ("The soul loves the body," Eckhart.) He traces the roots of creation-centered spirituality from the Jahwist books in the Bible, through to the 20th century.
In the chapter on panentheism, Fox cites the mystic-prophets of the 12th to 15th century, including Hildegarde of Bingen, ("You are encircled by the arms of the mystery of God."), Mechtild of Magdeburg ("I saw – and knew I saw – all things in God and God in all things."), Meister Eckhart ("Everything that exists is bathed in God"), Julian of Norwich ("We are in God and God, whome we do not see, is in us.") pp. 88-92.

asking me if ever I had been quiet during a session. "Quiet?" I said. "You mean neither of us says anything?" Yes, she answered. That was what she meant.

I decided to be quiet. This lasted about thirty seconds, maybe a little bit more. I was too inundated with dream images. When it was time to talk about planting my tree, I went right into it, with falling leaves, deeper roots, reaching for water.

"It's absolutely right," said Keller. "Young trees are transplanted in autumn, and with their leaves and their hanging roots."

"You mean, a tree is replanted with its leaves, like mine in my dream?"

I was surprised and deeply stirred. I had never thought that trees were replanted with their leaves. I imagined them leafless, all dark, without life, with the roots bundled up in a burlap bag. I had been given a dream which was more knowledgeable than I.

"It's also absolutely right, because it's your tree, a tree from America. A maple tree."

I was planting an American tree. I liked the idea.

"And the leaves will fall…" said Keller. The branches will be barren, and the tree will look as if it is dying. There will be an aura of sterility around it.

Will I be able to accept this inactivity, and still harder this appearance of emptiness? This was exactly what was worrying me. Suppose my roots could not reach the water? But I had the image of my maple tree. I could hold on to it. I could accept life's cycle in the tree. There is a Vietnamese proverb that says, "When the leaves fall, they return to their roots."

I would try to accept the same cycles for me, the same periods of inactivity, in French they are called *les périodes mortes*, dead periods.

"All the time the roots are reaching into the earth," Keller said. While nothing might seem to be happening, my roots would be digging deeper into the ground. In my dream they had gone so easily into the moist earth near the pond. The tree was in contact with the earth. And so I would be in contact. I would reach down into what is underneath, what is not visible, what is unconscious.

"This may all be an interior attitude," he continued. I was not to expect sudden retirement. I would not be retiring from the workshop that winter, nor from my writing, nor from my family. But I would be looking differently at everything at the same time. I would let each season come, trusting life's cycles. This was the lesson from my tree.

One short dream, and a life's program. We had barely talked about the writer friend in my dream. I wondered afterwards if she were indeed the woman in our workshop, if she were a separate person. Or was she instead my shadow side, the side that waits and accepts. The side that I had pushed away, thinking it pure laziness, pure putting-off to tomorrow, when I was racing for high grades, for achievement and recognition. Could my writer-friend be showing me a whole different perspective, one that my conscious ego has a hard time accepting?

In writing down my dreams and living with them, I learned that there is never only one reading. Dreams remain alive if we go down to them in our imagination. They die if we pull them up to our intelligence and expose them to too much cerebrating. It's like pulling a plant out of the earth and leaving it in the sun.

James Hillman, in *The Dream and the Underworld*, writes "It is not what is said about the dream after the dream, but the experience of the dream after the dream." For a dream to be kept alive, Hillman suggests that we hold on to its images. "It is better to keep the dream's black dog before your inner sense all day then to "know" its meaning."[31]

And so I carried my maple tree in my heart. Throughout the year, it spoke to me and took me deeper into understanding pain and anger. May Sarton in *Journal of a Solitude* wrote, "I think of trees and how simply they let go, let fall the riches of a season, and go deep into their roots for renewal and sleep." She wrote this when she was my age, 58 years old, wanting to tell the truth about her year of solitude. She realized she had idealized the experience in an earlier book, overlooking the pain. "The anguish of my life here – its rages – is hardly mentioned. Now I hope to break through into the rough rocky depths, to the matrix itself."[32]

Sarton tells me how to look into the depths. Much of my writing has avoided the anguish. If I can imitate the tree and learn to let go, then I can acknowledge the pain, knowing that I will recover. When I write about leaving

31. James Hillman, *The Dream and the Underworld*, Harper and Row, New York, 1979, p. 122. In this dense book, Hillman relates our dreaming life to the dark side of the soul. He sees dream-work as soul making which like any other imaginative activity requires crafting. "Our dream-work takes the term depth psychology to its logical and most serious consequences. The dream has led us back from Jung to Freud and then to a romantic tradition before Freud that can be expressed by the following fragment of Heraclitus 'When we are alive our souls are dead and buried in us, but when we die, our souls come to life again and live.'" p. 132.

32. May Sarton, *Journal of a Solitude*, Norton, New York, 1977, p. i. "My own belief is that one regards oneself, if one is a serious writer, as an instrument for experiencing. Life – all of it – flows through this instrument and is distilled through it into works of art. How one lives as a private person is intimately bound into the work. And at some point I believe one has to stop holding back for fear of alienating some imaginary reader or real relative or friend, and come out with personal truth." p. 77.

Carolyn Heilbrun (*Writing a Woman's Life*, 1988) called this book a watershed in woman's autobiographies because she deliberately retold the record of her anger covered by her book, *Plant Dreaming Deep*.

America and moving to France, I can begin to recognize that it wasn't always easy, that sometimes it hurt, that I felt altered and alone.

I can say that I lost my language, "the spontaneous flow of inner language, the eroticism of conversation, the free streaming of speech."[33] There were some things that no longer had the same meaning, my laughter had a different accent, and when I wanted to write in English, I no longer had the words. How could I write without my own language?

I can also say that I lost my identity. Was I French or American? There was something schizophrenic about living the experience. When I woke in the morning, would I live my day as an American woman or as a French woman? Some mornings I felt neither. The Italian director Fellini in one of his last interviews explained why he had always refused to make a film in America. He said it was because he didn't know the culture. "I wouldn't know what color to give the man's tie. In Italy I know." Did I know? In America? In France? In Switzerland?

Taking example and inspiration from my tree, from all the trees in my yard, I can let the leaves fall and go deep into my roots for renewal. The tree will be stronger. As in my dream, when I return to the pond another year, the open space will be filled. There will be new growth bordering the pond.

Or maybe the new growth will come more slowly. Time can not be counted. A year in dream language is symbolic. Maybe the branches aren't ready. Maybe the third volume

33. Eva Hoffman, *Lost in Translation,* Penguin Books, New York, p. 107. Hoffman left Poland to settle in Vancouver after World War II. "The worst losses come at night... I wait for that spontaneous flow of inner language which used to be my nighttime talk with myself. Nothing comes... This interval before sleep used to be the time when my mind became both receptive and alert, when images and words rose up to consciousness... spinning out the thread of my personal story." p. 107.

of *Offshoots* will take longer. Maybe my own writing will deepen still more slowly, seemingly sleeping, lying fallow.

"Everything is gestation and then bringing forth. To let each impression and each germ of a feeling come to completion wholly in itself, in the dark, in the inexpressible, the unconscious, beyond the reach of one's own intelligence... There is here no measuring with time, no year matters, and ten years are nothing. Being an artist means, not reckoning and counting, but ripening like the tree which does not force its sap and stands confident in the storms of spring without the fear that after them may come no summer."

Letters to a Young Poet, Rainer Maria Rilke[34]

34. These letters, which Rilke addressed to a young, unknown poet between the years 1903-08 speak to all writers. "There is only one single way. Go into yourself. Search for the reason that bids you write; find out whether it is spreading out its roots in the deepest places of your heart ... Then draw near to Nature. Then try, like some first human being, to say what you see and experience and love and lose." Rilke, *Letters to a Young Poet*, W.W. Norton, New York, 1962, pp. 18-19.

6. Feminine Mandalas

I am talking to a small workshop of women about writing. I close my eyes and try to continue teaching. Lucie is at my right and is listening to music. I ask her to turn it off so the women can hear me. The music continues. My eyes are still closed and I cannot open them. I ask her again to turn the music off so the women can hear me. She answers but I can't understand her. I don't even know what language she is speaking.

Finally she turns off the music. I open my eyes. The women are no longer there. I ask Lucie where they are. She answers but again I don't understand. I ask her to speak more slowly. She tells me that the women have left to visit the upstairs of the house. They will return to play bridge or backgammon. I say I don't want to play bridge or backgammon. I want to talk about writing.

(December 14, 1991)

I woke up extremely frustrated from this dream. It was early December, and I had just returned from New York where I'd given a workshop to a small group of women writers. I belong to an international guild of women writers and give workshops at their week-long summer conference. The winter workshop which preceded this dream was a one day gathering in a lovely guest house near the Hudson River. As I think of it now, some of the women did indeed visit the rooms upstairs. It is extraordinary, how a dream can stay alive and how when we go back to it, we can discover something more.

A mandala vision celebrates the tree of life.
(Hildegard of Bingen, 12th century, Rhineland)

This is the background. At the time of the dream I thought that I would continue to lead workshops of women writers both here in Geneva and in New York. Then I had this dream, about trying to teach with my eyes closed. I woke up feeling thwarted to say the least.

Yet something about the whole dream made me laugh. Here I was, thinking I was talking about writing to a group of women when in fact the room was empty. The women were visiting the upstairs of the house and would come back to play bridge.

When I told the dream to Keller, he looked at me, his eyes lighting up, waiting to feel my reaction. I told him it was a humbling lesson about my teaching. That usually when I closed my eyes it was a way to focus my attention, but in my dream it was a way to let the women disappear.

"Don't go so fast," he said. "Tell me more about your daughter Lucie."

Disconcerted, I told him about Lucie, the dancer, who finished her baccalaureate by correspondence courses while dancing in Geneva and went on to dance in Paris. She is our youngest daughter, aged 23, now back in Geneva combining dance and university. "She identifies herself as a dancer," I said.

Keller said this seemed important, that the person in the dream who informs me that the women want to play bridge is a dancer.

"She is speaking to you as a dancer. Try to situate her message at this level."

He talked about dance and how it is heterosexual. Ballet, pas de deux, in its tradition, is male and female. Here in your dream, he continued, you are teaching a group of women. First you lose your sight, you do not see them well. Then you lose your hearing, you cannot hear yourself speak. And when Lucie speaks, you lose your understanding. You don't know what language she is speaking. He paused to appreciate this. Blind, deaf, and mute.

Finally when order is restored, the women have disappeared to visit the upstairs, the bedrooms. They will come back to play bridge or backgammon.

"When you are only with women," Keller said, "it is sometimes hard to write. It is sometimes easier to play games. When you are all the same, there is no pas de deux. There is no creativity."

This would explain my frustration upon waking from the dream. Somewhere it rang true. By moments I did feel blinded in women's groups. I needed balance. I needed perhaps Pierre at home or Robert Russell, the blind writer and teacher from my first writers conference, at one of the workshops.

I remembered writing for an International PEN Congress in Lugano in 1987, a piece about androgyny in literature. I had gone back to the story of creation in the Book of Genesis, the first account[35], telling how God created both male and female in His image, thereby revealing His own nature. God the creator is both and from this union comes the child. I referred to Coleridge who wrote that a great artist is androgynous, that all true art comes from the fusion of the masculine and the feminine within ourselves.

Where was the androgyny in my dream? Was Lucie, my daughter, trying to tell me that women's groups all alone were sometimes better at playing games than at creating?

---

35. There are two accounts of the creation. The most often cited is the second (Gn 2: 21-22), relating how Yahweh God built the rib he had taken from the man into a woman. The first account (Gn 1:27) is kinder to the woman: "God created man in the image of himself, in the image of God he created him, male and female he created them."

"When you have gotten rid of the other," continued Keller, "when you have only the same, there is a shadow which is destructive and life threatening."
He was speaking of all types of groups, not just a women's writing group. Anything which is all the same thing can not be fruitful.
"And it is your dancing daughter who tells you this, the daughter who is heterosexual by definition."
Lucie was indeed heterosexual. And I remembered telling her about the dream and hearing her laugh as she looked at me wide-eyed, almost as if my dream was hinting at something she had thought about some of my women's activity. So my dear dancing daughter was helping me to open my eyes.
I thought there was still time in the session to share another dream which I had following the night of my workshop dream. I asked if we could stop talking about creativity and androgyny – subjects which were making me feel a bit harassed – and talk about a very different dream. Keller nodded, sat back, put his legs on the low table between us, and listened.

> I am coming down a hill along the road we used to live on in Italy. I am going to meet a strong exceptional woman. At the bottom of the narrow road, there is a brown horse, warm, soft, loving and clean. I put my arm around him.
> He takes me to the woman's house. I realize that the woman and horse are living together. I go up the outside steps and enter a sort of court room where the exceptional woman is sitting at the head of a circle of women.
> I introduce myself to her and say that the horse showed me the way. I then introduce myself to each of the women in the circle.
>
> (December 15, 1991)

We were quiet for a few minutes. I wondered why I had changed the subject and gone to this other dream.

"How did you feel about the horse?" he asked.

"I felt comfortable about him. He was large and loving. I felt like putting my arms around him. I was happy to go with him and let him show me where to go."

"Right. A good feeling. The horse represents here the masculine. When there is an animal, it usually speaks of nature and instincts. And here the horse is both instinctual and masculine. He takes you to the exceptional woman."

Keller suggested that the dream was a continuation of my workshop dream. Here too there was a group of women, but there was also the masculine. The exceptional woman was living with the horse which is not very customary.

Yes, and strangely enough this had seemed natural to me, that they were living together.

"Living with the horse, she has combined both the feminine and the masculine within her. She represents in this way the true creative self."

So this very different dream was taking me right back to creativity and androgyny.

"And the horse is waiting to lead you to her."

I followed the horse happily, hugging it, feeling its strength and warmth.

"The dream is grandiose," Keller said, picking up speed. "Look where the exceptional woman is located. She is sitting in a courtyard in a circle of women, the symbol of the mandala. It represents here the wholeness of women when the masculine is integrated. A full circle not an empty room."

I liked the word mandala, it felt round just to say it. One of my recurrent childhood dreams was of a round room where I was happily living all alone. The walls were circular

like in a tower. My bed covered half the room – a semicircle
– and I spent the days reading and writing on my bed. Then
as I started studying Jung, I learned that the Sanskrit word
for my round room, for a "magic circle," is mandala. Jung
used this word to designate a structure of wholeness. a symbol of unity, of the archetype of Self.[36]

There was my round room, and there was also my water
jug with its circles of clay. Now there was a mandala in my
dream. A circle of women. Not a group of women disappearing to visit the upstairs bedrooms of the house, but a
circle of women sitting in a courtyard.

It was time to leave and I had more than enough to take
with me. I let my warm strong horse lead me back to my
house, my circular wooden staircase, to my quiet little
office, once my youngest son's room. It was not round but
almost, with a window to my left and to my right, looking
out into our trees and the green front yard.

I sat down at my desk – an old oak secretary – and
opened *A Room of One's Own* by Virginia Woolf. The words
could not have been more direct.

"It is fatal to be a man or woman pure and simple; one
must be woman-manly or man-womanly... Some collabo-
ration has to take place in the mind between the woman

36. "The self is not only the center but also the whole circumference
which embraces both consciousness and unconscious; it is the center
of this totality, just as the ego is the center of the conscious mind." C.G.
Jung, *Psychology and Alchemy*, Coll. Works, Vol. 12, p. 41 (Glossary,
Memories, Dreams, Reflections by C.G. Jung).
"The self is our life's goal, for it is the completest expression of that
fateful combination we call individuality." C.G. Jung, *Two Essays on
Analytical Psychology*, Vol. 7, p. 238 (Glossary, *Memories, Dreams, Reflec-
tions by C.G. Jung*).
"The self was the end of the harsh road of individuation and the
purpose of all one's seeking, for in that self one experienced the
presence of the author of the mighty activity that Jung called God."
Jung and the Story of Our Time, Laurens van der Post, Penguin Books,
London, 1976, p. 252.

and the man before the act of creation can be accomplished. Some marriage of opposites has to be consummated... The curtains must be close drawn. The writer, I thought, once his experience is over, must lie back and let him mind celebrate its nuptials in darkness."[37]

And so the woman writer must be woman-manly. She must reconcile the masculine and the feminine, either within herself or without, with her lover. And sometimes – oh wonder – both within and without.

I thought back and felt confident that my love for Pierre had not bound me, but given me a ridge pole, a balance, between masculine and feminine, enabling me to give birth to our children. Now I was trying to reach down more consciously to the center, to the dark soulful part of me which had so willingly encountered childbirth – crying out in pain as it brought forth new life. I wanted to put this part, along with the fright and darkness, into words.

I was discovering the deep feminine self and at the same time the strong masculine. At close to sixty years old, the loving brown horse was showing me the way to my unconscious creativity. The horse was a figure of the helpful animus, and the exceptional woman of the creative anima. I was learning to recognize both sides and in my dream to hold them together in my true nature. Here

37. Virginia Woolf, *A Room of One's Own*, Harcourt Brace Jovanovich, New York, 1989, p. 104. Woolf wrote this work in 1929 when asked to lecture at women's colleges on the subject of Women and Fiction. In wanting to encourage writing of genius, she is led to speculate that, just as there are two sexes in the natural world, there must be two sexes in the mind, and that it is their union that is responsible for creation.

"I went on to sketch a plan of the soul so that in each of us two powers preside, one male, one female; and in the man's brain, the man predominates over the woman, and in the woman's brain, the woman predominates over the man. The normal and comfortable state of being is when the two live in harmony together, spiritually cooperating." p. 98.

was the inner marriage of masculine and feminine, of animus and anima.[38]

I was beginning to imagine such a union, to understand it as vital to my creativity. I was beginning to wake up. I remembered a line from Maxine Kumin's poem, The Archeology of a Marriage, "When Sleeping Beauty wakes up, she is almost fifty years old." Many people thought that as a poet Kumin was exaggerating, that this awakening came earlier. But for some of us, the awakening comes still later.

I thought about our workshop. Where was our creativity? Were we awake? Were we sufficiently open to one another and to others outside our group – not just to men writers, but to other writers in general? Or were we perhaps becoming too much of the same thing? I asked myself these questions thinking of my workshop dream.

This touched upon the whole question of feminism. There is always a balance to maintain. When the creative, caring feminine is open to the world, she brings healing and transforms her surroundings. But when the feminine isolates herself, she is apt to see the other as her enemy and to polarize her surroundings. When women reach out beyond duality, they become strong together, circles of women, feminine mandalas.

Feminine mandalas. This is the image of my second dream, correcting the image of the empty workshop

38. John Welch writes, "Jung's theory of the anima and animus, the masculine and feminine in the human psyche, suggests the possibility of a rhythm in life. The androgynous person, the person of the inner marriage of the masculine and feminine, is energized by the interplay between the two poles. Alternatively active and receptive, the androgynous person flows with life in a give and take, a holding and releasing according to the moment." *Spiritual Pilgrims*, p. 183.

June Singer identifies the androgynous person as "sensitive to the aims of the Self, as expressed in the rhythms of nature and the sense of inner harmony that comes from being in tune with them." June Singer, *Androgyny*, Doubleday, New York, 1976, p. 333.

room. No longer is the I figure in the dream blindfolded. No longer are the women visiting the upstairs and then returning to play games. Instead the I figure is being escorted to her deeper creativity, there at the bottom of the hill in a courtyard where the women are sitting in a circle.

Feminine mandalas. It is the image of the woman writer. It is the image – her work spinning on the wheel – which Ursula Le Guin described in her poem, "The Writer on and at Her Work."

> "Her work
> spins unrelated filaments
> into a skein: the whorl
> or wheel turns the cloudy mass
> into one strong thread,
> over, and over, and over."[39]

39. Ursula K. Le Guin, "The Writer On, and At, Her Work, in *The Writer on Her Work*, edited by Janet Sternberg, Volume II, W.W. Norton, New York 1991, p. 210. Sternberg in the Introduction writes that the narratives of the writers in the second volume are different from those in the first volume, ten years earlier. "I began to recognize a direction to the change. The story of the struggle to become a writer was no longer at the core of many of these accounts. Instead, I found writers looking outward, women telling more expansive narratives about their engagement with the new territory that is the world." p. 13.

7. Dark Currents

I am trying to flee some dark, devastated country, with Pierre and other people. We walk over hills and fields, knowing that the border is close.

Then I find myself in a canoe, dug out of a tree trunk, sitting next to a strong woman. Other people are standing behind. We are swept along in a torrent of swirling dark water, going downwards, into an old medieval city, between flooded houses.

We arrive at the end of the torrent, against a high wall. I realize that on other side of the wall is freedom. I try to dig a small hole through the wall. I pick up a bar and pound it through. I see countryside. It seems we could push through and continue our flight.

I look again. There is a complete army, hundreds of Romanian soldiers, dressed in dark blue uniforms. The soldiers in front are kneeling on one knee, looking straight ahead, with guns aimed. I nudge the strong woman. At first she doesn't see them.

We start to back away, retreating through the village, going uphill. We find a hotel where Pierre is waiting for me. We are dirty and wet. I realize I do not have my two bags. The strong woman has hers and says I must have left mine in the canoe. I can try to go get them, but the hotel looks so white and clean.

As I am hesitating, two medieval men in dark clothes come to tell me something. One of them turns around. He has a message written on the back of his breeches. It is in a foreign language. I am sure it says to follow them to find my bags. I will have to go back into the dark water.

(December 27, 1991)

When I took this dream to Keller, I forgot my dream book in the car along with my journal. I had been trying to go to the session with fewer books under my arms, but I had not planned on going utterly defenseless. As I sat in the dark green waiting room, I was trying to get used to the idea, that this time I would go into his office without any books, without any armor to protect me.

And so it was. I quickly described the Christmas holidays, the house full of family, all our children, plus three young grandchildren, and four more on the way. There was the planning and cooking, and also the sitting back and letting the children take care of things. I felt that if I were changing, then they too would change.

Keller liked this idea. "And did they?" he asked.

"A little." The kitchen no longer cleaned itself up, instead I was sitting still at the table. So the children went in and did it. My middle daughter Katie came to me and asked if I was all right.

Yes, I was all right, and the Christmas holidays had gone well.

Then I rushed into my long dream, so vivid in colors, almost in smells of medievalism, with hints of alchemy. I retold my dream and started acting it out, swirling down the torrents, then kneeling on the floor like the Romanian soldiers in their blue uniforms. Keller placidly watched me.

"Why is this Romania?" he asked.

I explained that it could be any dark, devastated country, but in Europe. There was something Eastern European, something medieval about the dream, the landscape, the city, the costumes.

"What do the Middle Ages represent for you?"

"Darkness. famine, and also alchemy, something spiritual, less materialistic. Something that sifts out the gold from the Dark Ages, from the black torrent." Much of my

recent reading had touched upon alchemy, and I had
seen this dream as reflecting a *nigredo*[40] period in my life,
a blackening, a swirling down into darkness, into uncon-
trolled forces of nature, then coming up to the whiteness
of the hotel, its clean orderliness. But I didn't want to
depart from the dream. I said nothing more and waited.

Keller spoke more slowly than usual, more deliberately.
He said that sometimes when all seems well around us,
the personal unconscious opens into the collective unconscious and sends us a dream which reaches beyond
our own little world and touches upon the collective
world.

So he thought with my dream. The currents of black
water are pulling at the base of our civilization. In
Romania, in all the Eastern European countries, underneath the new economic freedom lies the same spiritual
bankruptcy of our Western countries, which is attacking
the foundations of these "new" states.

I wondered what such a dream could mean for me,
living in Geneva. Yet certainly I had felt the magnetism of
the dream at a time of relative calm in my own life. I told
him so, and said that I had appreciated the calm especially after having lived through the terrors of what AIDS
might have meant for one of my children.

I explained. Lucie, our dancing child, had finally
brought herself to have the blood test for the infection a
week or so before Christmas. The following day during
one of her classes at university, her professor had given

40. Robert Bosnak describes three stages of alchemical images in our
dreams: the black image world is called the *nigredo* (leading to distilling), the white world is called the *albedo* (leading to transmuting), the
red world is called the *rubedo* (leading to transcendence). "The difficult process of the successful *rubedo* is that of bringing together and
keeping together the experiences of what we perceive as inner and
outer worlds." Bosnak, *A Little Course in Dreams*, Shambhala, Boston,
1988, p. 66.

her a copy of a new comic-strip book in French about AIDS, asking her how she would see the reception of the book in an English speaking environment. The book, titled *Jo*, was being distributed in Swiss high schools as an educational and preventive measure.

In the story, Jo, a young girl Lucie's age, persuades her boy friend, whose brother has died of AIDS, to have a blood test. She accompanies him and when they go for the results, it is she who is HIV-positive. Her parents are unable to cope. She moves in with her boyfriend and finally dies from AIDS.

Lucie identified completely with the protagonist. She stopped eating and sleeping. She showed me the book. She said she should never have had the test. She preferred not to know. Finally a few days before Christmas she asked me if I was worried. I said no. Then she asked if I would please call for the results on the 24th. She said she wasn't up to it. I felt I couldn't backtrack and agreed.

That morning I woke up dreaming I was on the phone with her doctor, who was also my doctor. I was even holding my hand to my ear as if cupped around the receiver. Quietly I went downstairs to telephone. It was still too early, not yet 8:00, the answering machine was on. I waited nervously, sitting by the phone while the rest of the house slept. At 8:00 I tried again. Still the answering machine.

I wondered if the nurse had forgotten to put the phone on. Perhaps they were not going to put it on, the day before Christmas. Finally at 8:20 I got dressed and drove to his office, less than ten minutes away. I explained to the secretary that my daughter had asked me to pick up the results. She checked with the doctor and told me this was not possible. I asked her to insist, saying that Lucie was traumatized with fear and had asked me to get them for her.

The secretary disappeared into the doctor's office. I waited. And waited. I couldn't believe they were taking so long. The secretary returned, again saying the doctor did not want to give the results. I tried to breath slowly, regularly. Then the doctor opened his door, crossed the hall, and without addressing a word to me, without even looking in my direction, entered the office of his secretary.

I couldn't believe it. Why hadn't he at least looked at me? Could it be? And still I waited. Alone in the hall. I walked in circles, ready to barge in on both of them and insist upon knowing. I thought about Lucie and the rest of the family still sleeping back home. I continued to circle around the hall. I imagined now the worst, tried to think it through. The secretary returned and handed me a sealed envelope.

"Give this to your daughter."

I looked at her. "Can't you tell me anything?"

"You can wish her a good Christmas. It will be a good one."

I burst into tears. Why had they taken so long? Why had my doctor not given me the envelope sooner? It was already after 9:00. I wanted to be home, to never see that office again.

I drove home, the house was quiet, only Pierre was awake and waiting for me. I told him the results. Then I went and knocked on Lucie's door. I leaned over her as she slept.

"Lucie," I said, "you're all right."

She shot up, tears already in her eyes. We hugged each other tightly and cried.

Lucie was well. But Joe – her counterpart in the book – had died. Why one and not the other? Who decides? How will we react when it is our turn? I didn't have any of the answers. I could only live each day.

I told all this to Keller, feeling again the terror and anguish of those hours. He answered me, no longer slowly and deliberately, but quickly and forcefully.

"Can't you see the depths of this, how you were pulled into the same black unknown currents as in your dream, how you went through the same movements in confronting the results, circling in the hall, tumbling down through the darkness?"

Indeed I had lost my balance. I had turned around in circles. I had wanted to scream with rage. AIDS is one of those dark underwater currents swirling below our society. This dream, this collective dream, echoed the depths of what I had lived through just before Christmas.

"You have an unbelievable capacity to belittle the difficulties you experience. You came in here today saying how happy and good the holidays had been. You weren't even going to mention this real nightmare."

Right. I wasn't going to mention it. I had pushed it aside, pushed the darkness away. I had made everything all right once again. My dream had brought it back. I could feel the swirling black torrents. I could relive my utter helplessness.

The time of my session was getting short. There was still the end of my dream, the two men in medieval clothes who had come to fetch me, with the message written on the back of their breeches. The seat of their pants.

I said it seemed vulgar somehow.

"Not vulgar but instinctive."

"Why?"

"These men, in medieval clothes, in breeches, will guide you back into the torrents, back into the dark, to your instinctual side. You can't just forget about the black water and live in the white hotel."

They were medieval because during the Middle Ages, body and soul were closer together. Julian of Norwich in the late 1300's wrote about "the glorious union" of body and soul.[41] Physical life and spiritual life were linked, reason was not so separated from imagination. All this came with the Renaissance, when reason seemed the highest goal, when man thought he could even reason God.

Now, my unconscious is taking me back to the Middle Ages, to nature, to my instinctual side, telling me to reconnect with nature, with the irrational, with Eros.

Ah, Eros, I thought. The breeches. Physical love.

But Keller wanted me to see Eros as much vaster. These two men were waiting to take me back to the dark unknown to recover my belongings, to become whole. Eros is a way of living, different from Logos[42]. It is relating rather than thinking.

Relating. This I understood. I told Keller I felt I related to lots of people, to family, to friends, to writers, to people at church, to people I meet.

"You do," he said. "But at the same time, you maybe think too much about it."

41. It was in her one book, *The Sixteen Revelations of Divine Love*, that Julian of Norwich wrote about the glorious union of body and soul, Mathew Fox, *Original Blessing*, p. 63. "God is the means whereby our Substance and our Sensuality are kept together so as never to be apart." p. 58.

Julian wrote her book because on May 8, 1373, she had a vision. "Our Lord showed me an inward sight of his loving... he showed me a little thing, the size of a hazelnut, in the palm of my hand, saying 'It lasts and ever shall because God loves it.'" Sheila Upjohn, *In Search of Julian of Norwich*, Darton, Longsman & Todd, London, 1989, p. 12.

42. Logos is the principle of power, meaning, and competence, the governing principle of the animus or the masculine aspect of the psyche. Eros is the principle of relationships, nurturance and relatedness, the governing principle of the anima or the feminine aspect of the psyche. See footnote 18, p. 45.

Peter O'Connor wrote that eros is "best conceptualized as a continuum, like a spectrum of light. At the one end is sexuality in its most primitive and least developed form – pornography ... At the upper end of eros is spiritual growth and development." O'Connor, *Understanding Jung, Understanding Yourself*, pp. 110-107.

I stood up to leave. This time I had no books.

"You see," said Keller, "your two medieval men are going to show you that Eros and Psyche are one. Love and the soul go together."

Yes, Eros had not only physically loved Psyche, he had helped her affront the underworld, enabling her to become god-like. She had gone down into the dark unknown.

In the days following, I went back to the myth told by the Roman writer Apuleius[43]. Psyche, the third daughter of the king, was so beautiful that she aroused the jealousy of Venus, who sent her son Eros (Cupid), the beautiful winged youth, to punish her. Instead he falls in love with Psyche and carries her off to his castle, coming to her only in the night and hiding his true identity as a god. Finally Psyche, encouraged by her two older sisters, lights a candle to see who he is. A drop of wax falls on the beautiful sleeping Eros. He wakes up and flees.

Psyche starts on her journey. She tries to win Venus to her side, completing three impossible tasks. But Venus assigns her still another task and Psyche must descend to the underworld, where she is overcome with sleep. Eros ultimately finds her and redeems her. Transformed through her journey, Psyche becomes a goddess and marries Eros as an equal.[44]

---

43. The myth is retold by Edith Hamilton in *Mythology*, New American Library, New York, 1973, pp. 92-100. "This story is told only by Apuleius, a Latin writer of the second century A.D. The Latin names of the gods are therefore used. It is a prettily told tale, after the manner of Ovid." p. 92.

44. Robert Johnson, in his book *She*, underlined the urgency of this myth for the modern woman. "The problem of Eros and Psyche could be condensed into a single word – levels. All of the journeys, tasks and struggles of Psyche are better understood by levels. She is thrown about between earth and heaven, mortality and immortality, humanness and godliness... All of her struggles are to reconcile the many levels which play upon her." Johnson, *She*, Harper Row, New York, 1989, p. 78.

I thought about another goddess who also descended to the underworld in the myth of Persephone and her Mother Demeter, Goddess of Grain. Without Hades, The God of the Underworld who carried her off in his chariot drawn by black steeds, and without partaking of the pomegranate seeds, Persephone might still be innocently plucking flowers in the meadow.

Instead the young Persephone integrates her dark side and becomes Queen and Guide of the Underworld, showing the way to mediate between the two worlds[45]. And the grieving Demeter, reunited with her daughter, restores fertility to the earth and acquires a wisdom which honors life and death.

My dream mirrored these mythical journeys into the underworld. The dark torrents, the medieval city, the dividing wall, were all images of my unconscious. I had gone downwards with the strong woman, swept along in the canoe. I had affronted floods and escaped from an entire army. When I thought I was safe in the white hotel above the desolated city, two medieval men came to fetch me, with instructions on the back of their breeches.

---

45. "Persephone represents the ability to move back and forth between the ego-based reality of the "real" world and the unconscious or archetypal reality of the psyche. When the Persephone archetype is active, it is possible for a woman to mediate between the two levels and to integrate both into her personality." Jean Shinoda Bolen, *Goddesses in Everywoman*, Harper and Row, 1985, p. 203.

Thomas Moore takes us into the mystery of the pomegranate. "When we allow experiences of death to touch us and take us down, we come back with seeds of the pomegranate in us, that fruit that looks sunny and whole on the outside, and yet has a highly articulated interior and is filled with dark seeds that recall the underworld." Moore, *Care of the Soul*, p. 48.

I am to follow them. I cannot live above, in the white world of vision, clean and safe. The Romanian soldiers are still there, hundreds of them, organized and armed. I have to return and fetch my belongings. I will follow Eros back into the dark currents. And I will taste the seeds of pomegranate.

"The ground of the soul is dark," counseled Meister Eckhart centuries ago.[46]

46. Matthew Fox, *Original Blessing*, p. 133. Fox cites Eckhart as "the most profound and biblical creation-centered theologian of the West." The 14th century preacher used the image of sinking into darkness, into the depths to find God. "We are to sink eternally from letting go to letting go into God." p. 139.

Beyond the marshes are fields, trees, and stone walls.
(Childhood album, Briarcliff, New York, 1940)

8. Green Frogs

I am surrounded by little green frogs, hopping around me happily, maybe ten or fifteen of them. I sit down. There are fewer frogs but they grow bigger. They are now standing on their hind legs, looking at me and still hopping around. I try to catch them. Every time that I get one in my hands, holding it, a smaller frog pops out, leaving only the old skin in my hands. I try again, but again the frog hops away, leaving the skin behind. And still I try.

(January 23, 1992)

I woke up from this dream still trying to hold on to one of the frogs. I could see them, five or six green frogs strutting about, in front of me, almost teasing me, "Come on, try to catch us." And each time I tried, the frog would slip out of his skin and jump back to join the others.

It was winter time, I wondered why I was dreaming about frogs. Frogs were springtime. When I was a little girl, I lived in the countryside outside New York City on a dead-end road with a swamp and fields and low stone walls beyond. Each spring, in the wet marsh grass, I'd collect tiny tadpoles and take them home in tin cans to watch them turn into little green frogs. Then I'd take them back to the swamp where they were free. All spring long, the peepers would sing, a shrill song which I still identify with my childhood.

My dream appeared very light and unimportant, especially at a time when I was trying to read *Faust*. My son the

piano player had been urging me to read it for a long
time. On my last visit to the States, I finally looked for it in
the Cambridge bookstores where I spent hours every
chance I had when visiting my oldest daughter Cecile. I
chose the Norton Critical Edition of Goethe's *Faust,* one
of the longest, with its three hundred pages of verse
translation and another three hundred pages of notes. I
was reading it slowly, twenty pages or so at a time, then the
notes.

In spite of this academic approach, parts of the poem
glowed, sending fire through my veins. I wanted to understand more, Faust's wager with Mephistopheles, his communion with darkness, his descent into the underworld. I
wanted to stamp my feet with him and go down into the
depths. But then I wanted to be redeemed, before death,
through love. I was in other words becoming just a little
inflated[47] with Faust's mood:

> "I'll sound the heights and depths that man can know,
> Their very souls shall be with mine entwined,
> I'll load my bosom with their weal and woe,
> And share with them the shipwreck of mankind."
> Book One, lines 1771-1775

So all puffed up with Faust[48], I dreamed of frothy little
green frogs. When I went to the weekly session with
Keller, I wasn't going to mention the dream. I wanted to

47. "This phenomenon [inflation], which results from the extension
of consciousness, is in no sense specific to analytical treatment. It
occurs whenever people are overpowered by knowledge or by some
new realization." C.G. Jung, *Two Essays on Analytical Psychology,* Coll.
Works, Vol. 7, pars. 202-295 (*Jung,* Campbell, p. 104).
48. Edward Edinger notes that Faust is here striving for wholeness but
Mephistopheles warns him this wholeness is only for a God. "Faust
does not make a distinction between the ego and the Self and thus falls
into a grandiose inflation which must lead inevitably to a fall." Edinger,
Goethe's Faust, Inner City Books, Toronto, 1991, p. 31.

share my reading of Faust, my striving for understanding, for encountering the dark side of my being, my "Mephistopheles."

Keller nodded but didn't seem duly impressed. As soon as I was quiet for a moment, he said, "And what about a dream?"

Discomfited, I left Mephistopheles and put myself back in the middle of the green frogs, trying to catch them. I didn't need to look back at my dream journal, the sequence was so short.

The face of Keller lit up immediately and he looked like one of the frogs I couldn't catch. Or did he look like Mephistopheles? I didn't have time to share the comparison.

"Look at these frogs," he said. "They jump into the air. They are aerial creatures and represent the unconscious part of your psyche."[49]

"The psyche?" I questioned.

"Yes, all the non-physical elements which your consciousness is unable to comprehend, which your ego is trying to make intelligible."

My light silly dream. Frogs, instead of books of knowledge, instead of Faust's library. I wanted to catch one of the frogs, I wanted to capture it. I wanted to understand. A pact with Mephistopheles? No, just a grasp at each frog, each psychic ingredient of my mind.

"Each time you catch one of the frogs, it is already out

49. The psyche, as a reflection of the world and man, is a thing of such infinite complexity that it can be observed and studied from a great many sides...I would like to emphasize that we must distinguish three psychic levels: (1) consciousness, (2) the personal unconscious, and (3) the collective unconscious." C.G. Jung, *The Structure and Dynamics of the Psyche*, Coll. Works, Vol. 8, pars. 283-342 (*Jung*, Campbell, pp. 23-38).

"Its non-spatial universe conceals an untold abundance of images which have accumulated over millions of years of living development and become fixed in the organism." C.G. Jung, *Freud and Psychoanalysis*, Coll. Works, Vol. 4, p. 331 (Glossary, *Memories, Dreams, Reflections*).

of your hands. It is elsewhere. So it is with the psyche. When you think you understand, your psyche has already moved on to something else, to a different level. It too is elsewhere."

And so my dream was right on. Like Faust himself, I was trying to grasp the secrets of the universe. The frogs were daring me, "Go ahead, just try." And when I did, they slipped away, taunting me still more.

It wasn't going to be easy to sit back and let the frogs be. I had always wanted to understand. Now I had to learn to live with my frogs, live with what I didn't understand, live with what escaped me, with what was constantly changing, with the flux of every day.

I went about the rest of the week, I finished reading Faust, letting myself by moments be carried along by its story and poetry, without worrying if I understood. I felt very alive and full of enthusiasm. I wanted to be prayer-full, love-full, insight-full. From time to time I remembered my frogs or they remembered me. I would be wanting to make a prayer mine, to make a relationship mine, an insight mine, well-defined and written down. Then the frogs would start jumping.

Wallis, the poet friend whom I had met in Russia and who had encouraged me with my writing, was coming to visit from Parma, where she lives with her Italian husband. So many synchronistic associations were wrapped up in our two lives that it seemed only normal our friendship deepen.

We shared manuscripts and critiqued one another's writing. We talked late into the night. She went to one of the workshops I lead and read some of her poetry. We drove up to the small monastery on top of the Voirons mountains, the monastery where I often went alone, where I bought my earthenware water jug. We prayed together there as we had in the churches in Russia, long moments of silence, sitting in front of an icon of the Holy

Trinity, remembering the iconostasis at Zagorsk where Roublev painted his famous portrayal of this mystery.

We spent the last evening talking about dreams. She spoke of a butterfly dream, and I spoke of my frog dream. Wallis told me she had once seen a frog lose its skin. "It pulled it up over its head and ate it," she said.

I was astounded. Did frogs really lose their skins? Were the frogs in my dream doing something which corresponded to their nature and that I knew nothing about? Wallis insisted that such was the case. Some frogs shed their skins, eat them and get on with it. She suggested that this might be the reason why it's so little known in comparison to snakes who leave their skins behind them.

I imagined my frogs pulling their skins off over their heads like sweaters. And in the background I heard them peeping, the way they did in the swamp at the end of Ingham Road where I grew up.

Wallis left the next morning. I stayed enkindled, aglow with my frogs. Later that week at dinner, I shared my discovery and enthusiasm with my husband and friends. They too had never heard of frogs shedding their skins, much less eating them. They didn't want to believe me. We got out the encyclopedia and looked it up. I read, "When spring comes, frogs leave the holes where they have spent the winter..." Here was my springtime again, just around the corner. I read on, the eggs, the tadpoles, the adult frogs, and the last paragraph, "When a frog is growing, it often changes its skin, just as toads do. It pulls its old skin off over its head and eats it."

There it was.

When at the next session, I related my story to Keller, he was delighted. He too did not know that frogs shed their skins. He grinned with satisfaction. "This is fantastic. You see, how much we have to learn?"

We were back with my frogs, frogs that jump into the air, frogs that lose their skins. "And think about it, they are also amphibian. They live on both land and water."

This too was important. Keller related how in the Greek play, *The Frogs*, by Aristophanes, there was a chorus of frogs. The story is about Dionysus, the God of the Vine, who journeys down to the underworld to bring back one of the dead poets. His city is languishing without song and music. As he starts on his dangerous way, the frogs who live both on the surface and below, are able to guide him.

"Your frogs are there to help you. Just don't try to hold on to them."

And so my frivolous dream about frogs was going to take me into my depths. I didn't have to understand, to explain, to dissect, nor sound the complexities of man's mind along with Faust. I didn't have to catch my frogs and hold on to them, in fact it was not possible. Instead I had only to sit back and watch them.

They would show me how to live both on the surface and in the depths. They were images of a new consciousness wanting to be born – one which is ready to hop into the water, and to sing and dance at the same time.

> "Longer stronger
> sing in the sunny daytime
> as we wriggle and dive in the marsh-
> flowers blithe on the lily pads
> and when Zeus makes it rain
> in green escape to the deep
> water our song still pulses
> and bubbles up from below."

the Chorus of Frogs, the Rowing Scene,
The Frogs, Aristophanes[50]

50. *The Frogs* was produced at the Lenaia in 405 B.C. and won first prize. Aristophanes, *Four Plays*, Meridian Classic Printing, Penguin Books, Canada, 1984, pp. 499-500.

9. Witch's Spell

A friend arrives and while we are talking about something important, I realize I can no longer see. I tell her I
cannot open my eyes. She is intrigued. I explain that this
often happens.

Someone calls from the yard. We are upstairs in my
house. I see it is an old woman who looks like a witch. I do
not want to answer. I think she will go away. She will know
I don't want to let her in.

My friend tells me I should answer her. I look outside
and try to open my eyes. If I am to answer this witch
walking around in my yard, I want to have my eyes open.

(January 16, 1992)

This was an afternoon nap dream. I woke up feeling
that I had seen this old woman – old witch – before, but
not knowing where or when. The dream left a disturbing
sensation as if not finished, something was happening
outside, or on the other side of my closed eyes.

And I wondered how I saw the witch since my eyes were
closed. It was true that often in my dreams I had my eyes
closed and couldn't see. But this time I had my eyes closed
and I could see.

It was all the more strange because I was expecting a
visit from this same friend later in the afternoon. When
she came, I did not mention the dream to her. We had a
coffee and sat down to talk, to talk about "important
things" like in my dream – about her work as a therapist,
about our older children, about my writing. As she was
leaving, my shoulder started to hurt. By evening the pain

was very sharp. There was a precise spot in the articulation which burned and which immobilized my entire shoulder.

I had suffered the same sharp pain twenty years earlier and had undergone all sorts of treatments from acupuncture to cortisone injections. The doctors had said it was a severe attack of arthritis. It lasted two weeks. Since then that shoulder had not hurt again. I had however ten years later permanently injured my right shoulder and grown accustomed to its persistent ache.

Now it was again my left shoulder. By the time I went to bed it was searing with pain. I could not sleep during the night. In the morning I could not move my arm. I took aspirin and lay still in bed, but the pain did not let up. Finally in the afternoon I went to see my doctor.

There was no doubt about it, I had a sudden arthritis. Had I fallen? Had I pulled a muscle? These attacks, the doctor said, just don't happen. They're caused by a collision, a fall, or a blow. I could find no reason. He gave me a prescription for a pain killer and told me to return after the weekend.

The pain killer knocked me out. The soreness in my shoulder was less acute but I could not stand up. My son Chris and his wife came for supper. He looked at me and said I looked stoned. My pupils were dilated. I told him about my shoulder and the medicine. He asked if I wasn't psyched. I laughed and said I could feel the exact point of pain. Of course, I wasn't psyched.

I tried to sit through supper, but, nauseous and dizzy, I soon went back to bed. I couldn't even read. So I lay there and waited. Again I didn't sleep. The next day I continued to rest in bed. In the evening the pain disappeared and finally I found sleep during the night. The following morning my shoulder felt normal but I was still knocked out. I moved about the house like a sleepwalker not fully conscious.

All this happened between Thursday and Sunday. Monday I called the doctor to tell him it was finished. He was surprised that the attack should disappear just as suddenly as it had come, and again without any apparent reason. So much the better, he said with audible relief.

Wednesday I took my dream and my shoulder to Keller, my other doctor, the one who treats illness as in ancient Greece, following the tradition of Asclepius[51], the great physician, in whose temples thousands of sick people came for healing. After they prayed and sacrificed, they would go to sleep, lying in circles around a stone well, and their dreams would bring healing.

Keller wanted to know what my witch looked like. He didn't worry about my eyes being closed. I could still see her. She was ugly and old in a stereotyped way – bent over, dark and wrinkled – and had a brown blanket wrapped around her.

Keller nodded, evidently convinced that it was indeed a witch. He told me that a lumbago in German is a *hexenschuss*, a witch's stroke. Lumbago is lower in the back, but the witch's stroke had spread to my shoulder. I listened to him, a *hexenschuss*? I was astounded. A witch had perhaps given a blow to my shoulder, or cast a spell upon it? So my son had been right. I was stoned, I was hexed. I was indeed psyched.

Keller continued. The witch is a personification of nature, in its good and bad aspects. When the witch casts

---

51. Asclepius, written Aesculapius in Edith Hamilton's *Mythology*, was believed to have called back a man from the dead, and to have been punished by the gods for having "thoughts too great for man." Zeus, angered that a mortal take power over the dead, struck him dead with a thunderbolt. For full story, see pages 279-281.

a spell on someone, it's often because that person is not respecting her own true nature.

"You did not let the witch come into your house," he said.

That was right. I thought she would know that I didn't want her and therefore go away.

"You were too busy with other things."

"Yes with important things," I said, realizing the irony.

"You would not listen to her. You were not in touch with your own nature. And so she lay you low."

Until then I had hardly believed in witches and now I was supposed to believe that a witch in my dreams had gotten even with me. That because I did not let her in my house, she gave me such a blow that I had an attack of arthritis, which my doctor could not explain.

"What did she want?" I asked.

Keller repeated my question and suggested that I look at what she had obliged me to do. When we want to know the reasons for something, we should look at the ensuing situation, at the results. The witch had obliged me to stay immobile for three days on my bed.

The *hexenschuss* had stopped me from doing. My witch wanted me to slow down. But whenever I did less, my conscious, achieving ego always reacted, asking what was wrong with me.

"There's nothing wrong with you," he said. "Your witch wants to block you into inactivity."

Indeed she had. I had laid on the bed, unable to move my arm, unable to even read.

"You will have the impression of doing nothing, of being good at nothing. And this demobilization will force you to reconnect with your inner nature."

I wondered about this. By not doing, I'd reconnect with something interior?

"With your instincts," Keller said.

It was time to leave. I thought back, trying to remember when if ever I had acted on instinct. As a little girl, I tried to bite the hand of the babysitter. It was a sudden outburst. She was trying to make me be still. She telephoned to my parents who came home. I was harshly punished. Another time in second grade I picked a fight with the boy sitting ahead of me. I should have been in his place. Instead I was sent to the end of the row. I learned to discipline my instincts, to shut them away.

Now my witch was leading me back to my instinctual side, not the side that always stays up front, that always knows how to get ahead, but the side that stays in the dark, that doesn't have to win. I remembered Inanna, the Sumerian goddess of heaven and earth who went down to the underworld to find her dark instinctive sister, Ereshkigal, Queen of the Underworld.

The Descent of Inanna

Inanna, Queen of the Great Above, set her heart on Earth's deepest ground. Turning her back on Heaven, she stepped down. "But your safety?" anxious voices cried after her. "If I do not return, go to the Fathers," she called back, already at the first gate. "On my way to the funeral," she explained to the gatekeeper and the sandstone bars gave away. Then down she went – through mud that tore the gold from her ears, through granite arms that ripped the shirt from her breast, through fire that singed the hair from her head... Farther and farther down she hurled through emptiness that drank her blood. Until at last she stood eye to eye with Ereshkigal, Queen of the Great Below. That unpitying Eye froze her heart and dazed she stepped through its pupil ringed with skulls that chewed the flesh from her bones, as farther and farther she fell in the hollow Abyss."

Janine Canan, "Inanna's Descent"

This is the oldest known myth about the descent to the goddess, written on clay tablets in the third millennium[52]. Five thousand years ago, women were descending into their depths to meet their dark side, they were abandoning heaven and earth, all the false trappings and identities that served in the upper world, to meet the dark goddess of the Netherworld and reclaim their other half.

Ereshkigal looked with her eye of death at Inanna and impaled her on a peg, where she remained for three days and three nights, until her corpse was restored to life and she returned to the land above, no longer all sweetness and light, but reunited with her dark side, whole unto herself.

My witch – like Ereshkigal – had laid me low for three days and when I finally stood up, I moved like a sleepwalker. I was in touch with something utterly new to me, making me feel a different level of consciousness, making me see with my eyes closed.

I wanted now to keep that otherness, that other regard, to not become once again all sweetness and light. To be true to myself, to my whole self, I had to embody not just the traditional aspects of the modern, well-adapted woman, but also the darker aspects, the inner instinctive knowing that suffering and death exist.

52. This rendering of the myth of Inanna ("Inanna's Descent," Janine Canan) is found in Maureen Murdock's book, *The Heroine's Journey*, p. 102. The author relates the rest of the story, how when Inanna returns from the underworld she sacrifices people who do not support her new identity, indeed she sends her own lover Dumuzzi to take her place in the underworld.

From this situation, a new feminine is born, Dumuzzi's sister, Geshtinanna, offers to share her brother's time in the underworld, willing to endure the cycle of descent-ascent-descent, "accepting the dark, instinctive side which helps us find meaning in suffering and death as well as the light, joyous side which reaffirms our strength, courage, and life." p. 119.

I went about my days with a different vision, closing my eyes from time to time to focus again on a deeper level. I reread Sylvia Perera's *Descent to the Goddess*, rediscovering again what the witch had done to me.

> "The return to the goddess, for renewal in a feminine source-ground and spirit, is a vitally important aspect of modern woman's quest for wholeness. We women who have succeeded in the world are usually daughters of the father – that is, well adapted to a masculine-oriented society – and have repudiated our own full feminine instincts and energy patterns, just as the culture has maimed or derogated most of them. We need to return to and redeem what the patriarchy has often seen only as a dangerous threat and called ... witch."[53]

I wanted to find again my early, instinctive embrace of life. I wanted to find those times when I used to sit very still alone outside on a rock, up a tree, near a brook, those times when I felt at one with myself and with the rock, the tree, the brook. The colors were so intense, the sky so completely blue, that I'd enter into a trance and not move. Now as I started to sit very still again, outside in the yard or inside at the window, I started seeing deeper colors, a different blue in the sky, trees so green I entered them. It was as if my surroundings had changed in tone and intensity, no rather my senses.

I wanted also to find again the darker moments, to go back to the black hole – the black tunnel – that haunted my childhood. I remembered the death of my grandmother and not being allowed to approach her coffin, there in the middle of our living room, not being allowed

53. Sylvia Perera, *Descent to the Goddess*, Inner City Books, Toronto, 1981, p. 7. The author contends that only after the descent to the underworld and the return to our daily world, can modern woman meet modern man as an equal and establish "a true, soul-met, passionate and individual comradeship as equals." p. 94.

to see her one last time. My parents had sent me upstairs to my room. Death was not for children. I became terribly afraid of it. In my imagination, it became a black tunnel – utter nothingness, without feeling, without consciousness – where I would whirl forever and ever in darkness.

I was told that Jesus Christ had done away with death, "O death, where is thy sting? O grave, where is they victory?" (I Corinthians, 15:55) But these words gave me little comfort. By rejecting death, I was rejecting life. And by rejecting life I was rejecting myself.[54] Slowly, with great effort, I learned to will away the black tunnel. When it came into my vision, I pushed it away. I consciously denied its existence.

Now I wanted to face it, to go into it, to descend into the darkness, literally to lose myself in it, to familiarize myself with death. I saw the whole cycle of nature, birth – death – rebirth. Joseph Campbell in *Myths to Live By*, wrote, "Our depths are the depths of space."[55] My black hole was one among billions.

I saw Inanna daring to go down into the underworld in order to be reborn, to bring both worlds together. I saw her leaving her masks and costumes at each of the seven

---

54. Marion Woodman wrote about this black hole, "It is matter so wounded, so betrayed that it is dissociated from consciousness... Women feel so betrayed by their body that they try to take up residence in their mind... The black hole in many men is as black as it is in many women... Their matter is dissociated from their spirit." And she concludes, "Life cannot be fully lived without embodiment, nor can death be faced creatively." Woodman, *Leaving My Father's House*, Shambhala, Boston, 1992, p. 363.

55. "So that we are the mind, ultimately, of space. No wonder, then, if its laws and ours are the same! Likewise, our depths are the depths of space, whence all those gods sprang that men's minds in the past projected onto animals and plants, onto hills and streams, the planets in their courses, and their own peculiar social observances." Joseph Campbell, *Myths to Live By*, Bantam Books, New York, 1972, p. 274.

gates, shedding her identification with the upper world. I would follow her.

And then my witch came back in another dream.

> I am following someone, a dark robed figure, through narrow streets. The city looks medieval. I am pushing a baby in a cart. We are going very fast, down a long narrow passage. On one side is a river, on the other side is a wall.
>
> Then I am in the cart, with the baby, and an old witch is pulling me. We are going still faster. I have to pull in the baby's legs and arms so that they will not get pinched against the wall.
>
> Or am I the baby and do I have to pull in my own legs and arms? I am intent on going somewhere and I am glad the witch is leading me.
>
> (February 3, 1992)

This was one of those dreams that made Keller sit back and say, "*Excellent!*" He'd say it in French. It has the same meaning, but with a tint of surprise in it.

"It's very clear," he continued with enthusiasm. "You are now trying to follow the witch, but as you are pushing the child, it is rough going. You feel that the road goes down steeply, you have to go very fast."

Yes, I could remember the feeling of being out of breath. I was running down the road, pushing the cart and there was the river and the wall. The cart was heavy, the witch was going very fast. I couldn't catch up.

"Then when you become the child and the witch pulls you, the situation changes. You are intent on going somewhere and you are glad."

Yes, I was on a cart, I was being pulled, I was no longer out of breath. I could lean back and be comfortable.

"Remember, the witch personifies nature. So we could say that it is your inner nature now leading you, your instinctual side."

I could start rediscovering some of the instincts I had hidden away. I could go back into nature, near the rock, the tree, the brook, and let go.

Instead of stalking me in my back yard and casting her spell on my shoulder, the witch was now leading me down a long narrow passage alongside a river. I was glad, I was not afraid. I was intent on going somewhere.

The *hexenschuss*, the spell of the witch, was transforming me. As I let go and let the witch lead me, I was becoming one with the child. I was the child. I was reunited with what I had left behind, suppressed, hidden – feelings of rejection, anger, aggressivity, desire. Like Inanna, I went down and found my dark sister, my instinctual side. And as I reconnected, I became one also with the witch.

I was for a moment – the time of a dream – all three. I was myself, my conscious self, my masculine driven ego, the person with her eyes closed. I was also my witch, my unconscious self, my darker feminine side, following the narrow path alongside the river. And I was my child, my creativity, my new awareness, glad and intent on going somewhere.

10. Squaring the Circle

I am upstairs in our old house in Briarcliff, New York, where I grew up. There are many people milling about.

I leave my parents' room and go into the small bedroom to get my child, who seems to be Peter at one year old. He is standing up in his crib, watching all the people. He recognizes me and holds out his arms.

He has been there a long time and needs a bath. I hug him and carry him to the bathroom where I run a bath. He goes into the warm water happily. I kneel down by the tub to wash him.

(January 24, 1992)

I loved this dream. I was back home, in the house where I grew up, the one near the fields, the maple trees, the swamp and the green frogs. My parents were there. We are all there. And Peter our first son is in his room. He holds out his arms to me. I kneel down beside him to wash him.

It was January, the dead of winter, the coldest month, yet the nights were already getting shorter. The dream seemed to be warm and kind, looking ahead to spring. I felt it was saying that all was well. I saw my son Peter as symbolizing my creative self, my writing. The dream was telling me to now turn inward. To return to my writing. And to honor my writing. The child in my dream has been in his crib for a long time but still he recognizes me. It's time to take care of him. He needs to be washed and brought out into the open.

To bring out into the open. These words took me back to a dream and an experience I had a few months earlier, in November while I was traveling in Russia on a writers tour for two weeks. At the time I wrote it down by hand in my journal.

It was 3:00 in the morning. I was in Odessa on the Black Sea. The white curtain rippled back and forth at the window of our hotel room. Outside I could see the silver onion-shaped domes of a large church. We had tried to visit it, finding everything sealed, until we came upon two makeshift doors which opened into a courtyard. The inside of the church had been converted into apartments. It was only a church on the outside.

Here is the dream.

> I am taking care of many people in our house in Geneva, including our grown-up children. As they get ready to leave, I remember I have also a baby to take care of. I go get her in her crib in the downstairs bathroom. She is awake, happy, standing up in the corner of her crib, but there is some blood on her arm.
>
> I look all over her body and find only a few scratches on her arm. Then I see that there are several straight pins stuck in the sheet of her bed. She could have hurt herself badly. I do not remember putting them there. I show her to the others. She is all right.

(November 7, 1991)

This dream had remained shadowy. I wanted to tiptoe around it. Was it the setting of the hotel room in Odessa, the setting where I had dreamed it? The white curtains, or the silver onion-shaped domes of the church? Perhaps the church which was no longer a church was reflected in my dream by the mother no longer a mother, the mother forgetting her child.

When I came back to Geneva and put my journals together, I went back to the last pages I had written before flying to St. Petersburg. It was about the transcendent function, the holding together of opposites and the emergence of a new consciousness[56]. Jung called this new consciousness our inner child. I had ended my journal entry with the cryptic words, "Bring child into the open."

This was the experience that I recalled now. Upon my return from Russia two weeks later, I had forgotten about these words. I was startled reading them anew, so strongly did they prefigure my dream in Odessa. There in my own handwriting was the message of my dream, "Bring child into the open."

Wallis, the poet whom I had met on this trip and with whom I spent long hours had been telling me the same thing. She had given me a beautiful image, saying that our writing was like opening the curtains in front of the altar, each time another curtain, another veil, going inside to the Holy of Holies. "Don't draw back," she had said, "go to your heart."

So in early December I had taken all this – my dream, my journal, my friend – to Keller who confirmed my thinking. My child that I was forgetting, that I had left in her crib, seemed strongly to represent my creativity. I was now to bring it out into the open.

"And remember," he said, "when finally, at the end of your dream, you decide to show your child to the others, she is all right."

"But what about the scratches on the arm and the pins on the sheet?" I asked.

56. "The transcendent function arises from the union of conscious and unconscious contents... The confrontation of the two positions generates a tension charged with energy and creates a living, third thing... a birth that leads to a new level of being, a new situation." C.G. Jung, *The Structure and Dynamics of the Psyche*, Coll. Works, Vol. 8 (*Jung, Campbell*, pp. 278-298).

"There is no violence here. There is only forgetful-
ness."

"But still, there are scratches, and pins stuck in the
sheet."

He suggested that the pins might represent the mother's fears about the identity of the child, her anxieties,
everything which binds and holds back the child.

The archetypal mother[57], he said, wounds her child.
Not only are you anxious about your child, your creativity,
but so is your mother anxious about you and your creativity. A child's creativity threatens the mother, and so in
some unconscious way your writing threatens your mother. Her fears are imaged in the pins which scratch your
arms.

I was listening intently.

Keller said that he sensed in this dream my difficulty to
enter into the identity of the writer. "You doubt it constantly."

This was true, I was forever trying to convince myself I
was a writer, forever seeking the approbation of others. It
was hard to say, Yes, I am a writer.

"But your poet friend says to look within. Your writing
voice is there."

I wondered about these traces left by my mother. I went
home thinking about the mother archetype, trying to
separate the Mother from my mother. My mother had
always encouraged me, echoing the voice of my father,

57. "The mother archetype was represented on Mt. Olympus by
Demeter, whose most important roles were as mother (of Persephone)
and as provider of food (Goddess of Grain) and spiritual sustenance
(the Eleusinian Mysteries)... The mother archetype motivates women
to nurture others, to be generous and giving, and to find satisfaction
as caretakers and providers... The destructive aspect of Demeter is
expressed by withholding what another person needs. She experiences
her child's growing autonomy as an emotional loss for herself." Jean
Shinoda Bolen, *Goddesses in Every Woman*, pp. 168-76.

"Be the best." She set high standards and expected me to meet them.

Then I had moved to Europe, putting 4,000 miles between us. Ten years later, my parents moved from New York to Phoenix, doubling the distance. When I started writing full time, Dad was dying from cancer. Mother was entering a long period of grief and depression. I realized I didn't really know what my mother thought about my writing

Perhaps she did feel anxious about what I had become – French, Catholic, mother of six, writer – and of what I might be writing about. Perhaps the pins in the sheet were real and were holding me back from a deeper creativity. If I could reconnect with my mother, it would bring new balance into my life, and I could reclaim my writing. In the words of my journal, I could bring my child into the open.

After Russia and this dream, there was Christmas, and all the children and grandchildren came home. The house was full. I dreamed of moving, of trying to pack, of having too much, of getting into the elevator with my hands full of the family silver and descending to the cellar. I had so much stuff in the elevator, I was stuck and couldn't reach the door. I was jammed in the elevator.

Where was my inner child?

Weeks passed.

Eureka – the wonderful word which Archimedes used on discovering a way to determine the purity of gold – my unconscious gives me a dream of my childhood house in Briarcliff where I am leaving my parents room to take care of Peter our first born.

And the child hugs me.

I was happy to share this with Keller – the recent dream, with the child in the warm bath, along with the older dream, with the child in the crib and the pins in the sheets.

"See how the two dreams go together," he said. "Every time this happens I still sit back in wonder. And see how much further goes the second one. This time you are back in your parents house and you are leaving their bedroom to take care of your first son."

The symbolism was clear. My parents, like the king and queen in so many fairy tales, represent my old consciousness, my old way of seeing things. I leave them and go to my son, not a daughter but the divine child, who has been waiting a long time and who holds out his arms to me.

"Yes," I said, "he was happy to see me."

"He was so happy that he lets you wash him, and he goes easily into the warm bath which you have prepared. There are no more pins scratching him."

I remembered kneeling close to him, washing him.

Water, the source of life, of healing, of rebirth. There was all this. The pins were gone. I, with the child, found wholeness. At the same time that I was looking back and reconnecting with my childhood, I was looking ahead and taking care of my inner childhood, my own creativity.

It was an Epiphany dream, I was ready to celebrate the birth of my Savior. And then came still another dream in this series, a dream in three short parts.

> I am carrying something around the four bases of a baseball field, first, second, third and then home.
> I am again carrying something this time around the four points of a circle.
> And now I am carrying a baby, a one-year-old in my arms. The child is looking straight forward. We walk around the circle, first to the north and south, then to the east and west, to the four points of the circle. I feel as if I have succeeded.

(January 26, 1992)

With the Divine Child comes new consciousness.
(Icon of the Nativity, Chevetogne, Belgium)

When I started to write this dream, I only remembered the first two parts. I woke up fully awake and went to write them down on my computer, even though they were so short. Then the third part came back, with the distinct memory of the child – a one-year-old – and of the four directions – north, south, then east, west.

Keller appeared energized by this dream. "Explain to me, your game of baseball," he said, leaning forward.

I explained how the game was set up, the diamond, the four bases, how two teams played and the player who hit the ball ran around the bases. I described how it was very much of a team sport.

"It's very American, this game. It's extraordinary how this dream reflects the cultural environment of your childhood."

This was important, Keller suggested, as he shared his thoughts about this "mighty dream of transformation." My new consciousness was no longer forgotten, left behind in a crib. It was now washed and dressed and taken into the world.

"Here is what Jung called the divine child, born out of the *coniunctio* of the personal conscious and the collective unconscious, of the ego and the Self."

His words touched down deeply inside me, making me almost afraid. I had read about *coniunctio*[58], trying to first just say the word, then to understand it, union of two

---

58. Edward Edinger writes that from the *coniunctio oppositorum* (the union of opposites) comes consciousness. "Gradually the individual becomes able to experience opposite viewpoints simultaneously. With this capacity, alchemically speaking, the Philosopher's Stone is born, i.e., consciousness is created. The Philosopher's Stone is often described as the product of the *coniunctio* of sun and moon... the sun corresponding to the conscious psyche and the moon to the unconscious... It is a product of a *coniunctio* often symbolized by the union of the red king and the white queen, the king and queen standing for any or all of the pairs of opposites." Edinger, *The Creation of Consciousness*, pp. 19-20.

opposites, of light and darkness, sun and moon, the conscious and the unconscious. In alchemy, this *coniunctio* gives us the philosopher's stone, which is a symbol of consciousness. Now Keller was using this word in reference to my dream.

"The dream is anticipatory," said Keller, as if sensing my uneasiness, "its timing is not defined."

I breathed more easily. I was not holding the philosopher's stone in my hand. Keller understood and smiled. It wasn't that simple.

"You know, Jung would very much like this dream. The divine child, the circle, the mandala."

He explained again how Jung had noted the tendency of the human psyche to use a circle to express wholeness. "The mandala is the path to the center."[59] In dreams the mandala seems to indicate inner peace, it is a glimpse of the deeper Self. And the quadrangle, the baseball field, symbolizes a new and conscious realization of this inner wholeness.[60]

---

59. Jung wrote "When I began drawing the mandalas, I saw that everything, all the paths I had taken, were leading back to a single point – namely to the mid-point. It became increasingly plain to me that the mandala is the center. It is the exponent of all paths. It is the path to the center, to individuation... I began to understand that the goal of psychic development is the self. There is no linear evolution, there is only a circumambulation of the self... I knew that in finding the mandala as an expression of the self I had attained what was for me the ultimate." *Memories, Dreams, Reflections by C.G. Jung,*, p. 222.

60. Aniela Jaffé wrote about the squaring of the circle in the arts, contending that the separation of the circle (symbol of the psyche) and the square (symbol of earthbound matter) is a symbolic expression of the psychic state of the 20th century man. If today the two seem dissociated, they were not always so. "The contradiction can be understood also as a symbol, namely as a visual representation of the mathematically insoluble problem of the squaring of the circle, which had greatly preoccupied the Greeks and was to play so great a part in alchemy." Jaffé, "Symbolism in the Visual Arts," *Man And His Symbols*, edited by Carl Jung, Pan Books, London, 1964, p 272.

"In your dream, you take your new consciousness, and go across the circle, the diamond, north to south, east to west."

Keller talked about each direction. North was like home base, our first consciousness, where we come from, my childhood house. Then we go south, to Africa, to the dark continent, to what we don't know about, to the unconscious. Next to the East, we face the rising sun, the clarity, everything to the right of the Nile, the temples, life celebrating life. The direction here spoke to both of us. Keller chose carefully his images, we had both at different times traveled in Egypt and had talked about the river. Then to the West, we face the setting sun, the tombs to the left of the Nile, the non-doing, death, the place of new birth.

I was fascinated. My dream which had seemed so short, a few lines, had taken me from home to Africa, from temples to tombs, from sunrise to sunset.

"You have squared the circle," Keller said, standing up to emphasize the conclusion of my dream. It was time to go home.

I carried my circle and my baseball diamond with me. My circle was whole and round, an image of my inner Self, the unconscious Self. At the same time it was a diamond, with four directions. I knew that a circle couldn't be a square, nor a square a circle. It was impossible. Yet in my dream it was real and it was possible.

The two held together, like on the Tibetan tantra hanging in Keller's office, the perfect mandala, the circle in the square.

"A mighty dream of transformation…"

11. Windmills and Pigs

I am getting ready to leave a place. I am with other people. We are standing outside on a hillside when many of the people are turned into windmills. I see the windmills revolving.

Then as I walk away, the other people are turned into pigs, large, healthy looking pigs. I am not frightened. It all seems normal.

(February 1, 1992)

This dream seemed like nonsense to me. Windmills and pigs. What rapport? I could still see the hillside of my dream covered with windmills. They resembled windmills in Crete or Cyprus, wooden structures, not the solid stone ones in Holland. The pigs were there, fat and happy, clean and comfortable looking. I was not upset nor frightened. It was all right. Nor was I distressed that the people who were with me had been transformed into windmills and pigs. But I could make no sense of it.

When I went to see Keller, I was not thinking about the dream. I wanted to talk about the week and my growing frustration as I tried to understand what was happening around me. I had felt out of touch with people during the week, in my family, with our friends, in my writers workshop, and at church. I was no longer relating. I was no longer sure of my direction, of where I was going.

Keller told me that everything was all right as it was. I should let everything be.

But I wanted to know if I was going in the right direction, doing the right thing.

He told me that my doing was now to be a non-doing. By wanting to always do the right thing, I was losing myself. He reminded me of my witch and how she had cast a spell on my shoulder, trying to slow me down. And of my green frogs. I couldn't hold on to them. They popped out of their skins. So it was for what was happening around me. I should let go.

"I don't mean," he said, "that you should let go of your husband, your friends, your writers workshop, your church. Of course not. I mean let go of your old attitudes, the way you used to look at everything."

I remembered my windmill and pig dream. It seemed suddenly to relate to this letting go. I shared it with him, reading it from my notes, almost embarrassed about its evident lack of depth, still wanting to belittle it.

"Wait, something's interesting here." He stopped and looked at me, narrowing his eyes and nodding his head. "Windmills, they are receptive to the air, the wind. And pigs are receptive to the earth."

I could agree with this but I didn't know where it was leading me.

"The air, the wind, is a symbol for the spirit, for the yang force. And the earth is a symbol for the feminine, for the yin force.[61] As you move on, these forces are being activated. Parts of yourself are turning with the wind, are receiving strong yang power, other parts are hugging the earth, drawing strength from your feminine side, more yin oriented."

So I was now part windmill and part pig. As so many other times, I sat back and listened, realizing once again that I had been ready to discard a dream, thinking it rather foolish, but no, it all fit together – my anxiety, the

61. In the Chinese world order, yang and yin represent the masculine and feminine principles, the active and passive, the light and dark. See footnote 76, p. 139.

questions I was asking, and the dream that I was working with.

Indeed I did feel dizzy by moments, my head turning. With a flash I realized at the same time that I felt drawn downwards, wanting to sink and experience darkness. I was so often closing my eyes. I remembered speaking to Keller about this attraction to the earth. I remembered quoting that line from Faust, when Mephistopheles says, "Sink down by stamping, and stamping you will rise." There I was stamping on the hillside with the pigs.

"This dream is not so little," Keller continued. "It's a lesson in individuation."[62]

He said there were three levels of individuation. The first he called socialization. In discovering ourselves, we either conform to our surroundings or we confront them. In either case there is socialization. In the second level, our social masks no longer fit. New archetypes are being constellated. They are still passive but they are changing our outlook. We feel out of place. We lose our footing.

62. "I use the term 'individuation' to denote the process by which a person becomes a psychological 'individual,' that is, a separate, indivisible unity or 'whole.'" C.G. Jung, *The Archetypes and the Collective Unconscious*, Coll. Works, Vol. 9, p. 275 (Glossary, *Memories, Dreams, Reflections by C.G. Jung*).

"But again and again I note that the individuation process is confused with the coming of the ego into consciousness… Individuation is then nothing but ego-centredness. But the self comprises infinitely more that a mere ego." C.G. Jung, *The Structure and Dynamics of the Psyche*, Coll. Works, Vol. 8, p. 226 (Glossary, *Memories, Dreams, Reflections*).

"The individuation process, as understood in Jungian theory and encouraged in analysis, involves a continuing dialogue between the ego, as the responsible center of consciousness, and a mysterious regulating center of the total psyche which Jung called the Self." James Hall, *Jungian Dream Interpretation*, p. 21.

"Much of the Jungian analytical process consists in finding out a person's individual myth and then unraveling all the associations and feelings attached to it until one comes at last to the root metaphor or guiding principle." June Singer, *Seeing Through the Visible World*, Harper & Row, San Francisco, 1990, p. 12.

We're out of sync – how wonderful, out of synchronicity – out of an inner unconscious relating because we're not yet there.

This is where Keller said he would place my windmills and pigs. This would explain my feeling of malaise with the people around me, with my writing, the writers workshop, the parish, some of my friends.

"You don't fit in the same way. Your persona[63] is no longer the same. The status quo no longer holds. And your ego reacts. It wants to know what is going on, it wants to direct, to be in control."

My ego always wants to direct, to be in control. That was exactly what I was saying in the beginning of the session. I was frustrated because my ego no longer knew what was happening.

At the third level of individuation, Keller continued to explain, these new archetypes are active and release energy. They become laboratories in which the ego takes the four elements – air, earth, fire, water – and creates new consciousness, new life. Each time an archetype is integrated, our faculties of understanding are in turn enlarged.[64]

"This dream is right on target," said Keller. "You are leaving some place, not literally, but figuratively. You are discovering new ways of being. And so you dream of

---

63. "The term *persona* is really a very appropriate expression for this, for originally it meant the mask once worn by actors to indicate the role they played... It is a mask that feigns individuality, making others and oneself believe that one is individual, where one is simply acting a role... It is a compromise between individual and society as to what a man should appear to be." C.G. Jung, *Two Essays on Analytical Psychology*, Coll. Works, Vol. 7, pars. 202-295 (*Jung*, Campbell, pp. 103-104).
64. Emma Jung (edited by von Franz), in *The Grail Legend*, underlined the importance of these emerging archetypes pointing out that their integration brings about a change of attitude which is indispensable in the process of individuation.

people becoming windmills and pigs, and it all seems normal. You are not even frightened, at least not in your dream."

The lesson was clear. Things were moving so much that I was not surprised nor frightened in my dream. But I had been anxious and dissatisfied in my waking life during the week. My dream was there to help me move on. It was working on a level of me which was unconscious.

I went home with a feeling of new assurance. Maybe I could let go. I didn't have to always do better, do more. In fact I didn't have to "do." I could just "be," or I could try. Doing was one of my masks. I understood well that this was how I related to people around me. I did. At home I did. At the writers workshop I did. At the church I did. All through my life, I had always done. At college, way back, I did. I got married and I did. Six children later and I was still doing. The dream was now suggesting that I do no longer.

It seemed extraordinary that I could even consider not doing. I had had months of relative quiet – with husband busy and challenged by his work, and children all going their own different ways – which had let me focus on my reading and reflections, my dreams, my yearnings. It was a unique period in my life. Having loved, and lived with, Pierre over thirty years, having raised our children, this time of quiet was a healing.

I was the miller's daughter in the Grimms' fairy tale "The Handless Maiden" at the time that she had the lovely silver hands, fashioned by the king's son. I too had loved the king's son, given birth, and lived in his world with the king as protector. Now, like the princess alone in the woods with her son for seven years, I had the chance to live quietly in my own inner world, to go down to the source of my creativity, and to grow my own hands – not silver hands, crafted by silversmiths over the centuries. But my hands, a woman's hands, alive and creative.[65]

I thought about not doing. It was the end of winter. Spring was coming. I was asking myself questions about my writing, my editing, and about the workshop I was leading. The international group of women writers to which I belonged, and at whose summer conferences I taught, had asked me to write a profile of myself for their bi-monthly magazine. I was to answer the question, "Who am I?" with two pages of autobiography.

It was a difficult question for anyone, especially for a woman emerging from bringing up children in a foreign language and in a foreign land, a woman still looking for her own voice – her own hands. And still more difficult for someone dreaming of windmills and pigs. My old way of identifying myself no longer fit, and I didn't know what my new identity was. I wasn't ready to wear a new mask, especially in print.

I struggled over this piece of writing as never before. Was I a wife, a housewife? A mother, a grandmother? A woman writer? Why not just a writer? I was a writer. All

65. This fairy tale is found in the complete collection, *Grimms' Tales for Young and Old*, Doubleday, New York, 1983, pp. 113-118.

Marion Woodman in her book, *Addiction to Perfection*, wrote "The silver hands, which suggest an artificial Eros relationship because the instinctive spontaneity is not possible to her, can only be replaced by living hands when some miracle of love intercedes." pp. 145-147.

Julia Jewett in her essay "Womansoul," wrote "This seven year stretch in the woods is a period of deep introversion which is absolutely necessary to really get to the bottom of things, to really know oneself. And then she grows her own hands. She will have her own ground, her own standpoint, her own style, her own Self." Stein & Moore, *Jung's Challenge to Christianity*, p. 172.

Clarissa Pinkola Estés follows the handless maiden through seven stages of initiation in the Underground Forest, "When we come up out of the underworld after one of our undertakings there, we may appear unchanged outwardly, but inwardly we have reclaimed a vast and womanly wildness." Estés, *Women Who Run with the Wolves*, Ballantine Books, New York, 1992, p. 455.

right I thought, "Who am I?" "I am a writer." But I couldn't do it. I couldn't write it. I continued to sweat tears.

A dream came along, later that same week.

> "I am leading a group of women to visit an old castle on the outskirts of a city. It takes longer to get there than I expected. We get lost in the gardens and courtyards. At one point we have to cross a muddy stream. I am barefoot. I cannot see the bottom but the water is not deep.
>
> I walk into it. I cannot see my feet but it feels all right. I am still trying to find our way to the castle."
>
> (February 2, 1992)

Now in retrospect I see that this dream fit right in with what I was living. I wonder that it did not overwhelm me at the moment. It is amazing to go back to a dream and discover how much more it contains than what was seen at first. And it will always be so. In another year, if I go back to this courtyard and stream, the muddy water will speak to me in still another way.

Each one of these dreams is like a precious stone, standing and shining alone, yet fitting into a pattern which forms another, still more beautiful whole, like a mosaic of all colors and shapes. I imagine that our identities are this way, each one individual, yet fitting together into another design still more extraordinary.

But my profile?

When I went to see Keller the following Wednesday I was still struggling with it. He listened patiently.

"Am I a wife and a mother and a writer?"

"Yes," he answered.

"Or a woman writer?"

"Also," he said.

"Or could I be just a writer?"

"Why not?"

I was getting no closer to an answer so I switched to my dream, the castle, the muddy stream, barefoot in the water.

"Look," he said, "here you are with women following you, going to a castle, leading them to greater wholeness. And there is a muddy stream. Mud. Earth. Water. Darkness. You go right into it, without hesitation, even though you don't see the bottom of the stream. It feels all right. You can stand there. This is real. This is strong."

He was getting me excited about it. I could feel the water swishing around my ankles, the mud squeezing between my toes. He went on to explain. Before we can encounter new psychic growth, we have to accept not seeing our feet, losing our footing, walking in the imagination, the unreal.

"You're doing just that," he said. "And you're even leading along a group of women there. It's no wonder you are having difficulty writing about where you are, who you are. Your feet are in the water. You're penetrating into something new and unfamiliar, yet it feels all right."

Yes, it was unfamiliar, that was for sure. So it was all right. It was good. I was finding my way. This rang true.

"But not everyone is going to want to stick their feet into dark muddy water. What could be there? In the *I Ching*, it is written that the dragon, the creative force, is hiding there."

He stopped. "Do you know the *I Ching*?"

I said no. I had read about it. I had picked it up sometimes in a bookstore, hesitated to buy it, but always put it back on the shelf.

He explained a little about this old book of Chinese wisdom[66], which dates back over 5,000 years and reveals the patterns and secrets of life. Read and used as a way

---

66. "The *I Ching* does not offer itself with proofs and results; it does not vaunt itself nor is it easy to approach. Like a part of nature, it waits until it is discovered. But for lovers of self-knowledge, of wisdom – if there be such – it seems to be the right book." C.G. Jung, Foreword to the Richard Wilhelm Translation of *I Ching*, Penguin Books, London, 1989, p. xxxix.

to explore the unconscious, it works along the same lines as Jung's principle of synchronicity. In the same way that causality describes the sequence of events, so synchronicity – to some of us and to the Chinese mind – describes the coincidence of events.

I listened, intrigued, sort of on fire and enlivened. I believed in synchronicity, I often experienced it and felt that if we were awake to this interdependence of events, we would live on a very different level. Synchronicity was for me a way of seeing into my conscious everyday life, like dreams were a way of seeing into my unconscious life. It was a way of holding the two worlds together.

But there was not time to go further. I went home, excited about the newness of the situation. I went back over my dream and was again surprised that I had stuck my feet into that muddy water. Yet I remembered other similar happenings. I would be alone in the house, afraid of some noise, hesitant to go downstairs. Then suddenly I would follow an urge to confront the darkness, the beast, whatever.

I thought back to when I was a child, often I went off on my own, into the fields, the woods, alone, liking the feeling of danger. I'd stay home alone and explore the house in the dark. I went off to school alone, choosing to leave home at thirteen years old. I went to college alone, and to Europe alone.

I went to Grenoble and met Pierre. I fell in love, for the first time fully in love, with someone not speaking my language, someone as different from the blond, crew-cut brazen American boys, as night from day.

Then I had children. I was a mother. I was no longer my free self. I stopped doing things alone. I stopped stepping into the darkness. I grew very reasonable.

And now I was dreaming of stepping barefoot into dark muddy water, of not being able to see my feet, and of liking it.

Wallis, my friend living in Italy, was again coming for a short stay. She would bring me strength as a writer. I had reworked many of my essays, opening them, holding back less. I was trying to pull back the veils as she had suggested. "Don't just show us the iconostasis, but show us what is behind it." So I was working on my collection, going deeper.

We shared our writing – her poems and my essays. We laughed and cried, we felt again the excitement of discovering a kindred spirit, a friend whom it seemed we always had. It was a time of affirmation for me.

The last day of her visit, we went to the bookstore downtown, looking for one or two books. I don't remember the titles. While standing together in front of the shelves, I saw the *I Ching*. Wallis saw it at the same time and asked me if I had it. I said no. She picked it up and bought it for me. She'd help me do a reading that evening before she took her train to Parma the next morning.

Back home we sat at the dining room table, and Wallis explained how to consult the *I Ching*, how to listen to its wisdom as a guide in difficult life situation. We wouldn't find a yes/no answer. We wouldn't learn if we should do one thing rather than another. But if we place ourselves there on the path where it is difficult for the moment, the reading will help us find our way.

She asked me for three coins. Heads would indicate yang (in the sun), tails yin (in the shade.) I was to throw the coins three times, and then again three times, forming two trigrams. Each trigram had a meaning and when the two were joined together, the hexagram would correspond to the present moment in such a way that it would indicate what was essential in the situation, and thereby answer my question.

I threw the coins six times. We marked down each line, two heads and one tail made a young yin line. Two tails

and one head had made a young yang line. On the fifth
throw I had three tails, this was an old Yin line, ready to
change. I had my hexagram. It was number 64, with one
changing line. Then she left me alone, with the *I Ching*
and my drawing.

I looked for number 64, the last of the hexagrams. It
read, "Wei Chi/Before Completion." That sounded right
but I knew so very little about the book, about the way to
find its wisdom. The top trigram was called Li, the Flame,
Fire. The bottom trigram was K'an, the Abysmal, Water. It
said, "This hexagram indicates a time when the transition
from disorder to order is not yet completed."

I read on, curious about the image of fire over water.
"The image of the condition before transition. Thus the
superior man is careful in the differentiation of things, so
that each finds its place."

I had asked for confirmation of my writing, the direction it was taking, my collection of essays, my work with
the writers workshop. The *I Ching* counseled me to go
slowly. "This hexagram presents a parallel to spring,
which leads out of winter's stagnation into the fruitful
time of summer." I was back at the end of winter.

Fire flames upwards, it is a symbol of yang, active and
masculine, like the spirit of Pentecost above the heads of
the disciples. Water flows downward, the abyss can be
dangerous, it can also be receptive. It is a symbol of yin, a
symbol of rebirth, feminine and passive, like the waters of
baptism.

All night I read on. I went back to the beginning and
read Jung's Foreword to the *I Ching*, in which he explains
how he himself consulted the book when his friend
Richard Wilhelm asked him to write an introduction.
How could he introduce such a formidable monument of
Chinese thought? "While the Western mind carefully sifts,
weighs, selects, classifies, isolates, the Chinese picture of

the moment encompasses everything down to the minut-
est nonsensical detail because all of the ingredients make
up the observed moment."[67]

I looked back at my hexagram. Before Completion.
Fire over water. I was with the second pair of elements.
First I had dreamed of the wind and the earth with my
windmills and pigs, also a pair, also yang and yin. Now fire
and water. Keller had spoken of taking the four elements
together in the third step of individuation and creating
something new. I had asked the *I Ching* about where I was
heading, about my writing. It responded, "Before completion."

And the fifth line, the old yin with its three tails was
pointing to an inner tension and changing into a yang
line. No reading is unmoving, no situation in life is
unchanging. When there is too much yin, then the pendulum swings over to yang. This forms a new trigram. For
me, it becomes the trigram of heaven, the trigram of the
dragon, hovering above the trigram of water. The reading
was "Conflict. You are sincere and are being obstructed. A
cautious halt halfway brings good fortune." Had not
Keller told me that the dragon might be hiding in the
water?

Mystified, I let these images seep into my imagination
alongside the images of my windmills and clean healthy
pigs. Fire and water, wind and earth. New archetypes were
making me lose my footing. I was standing in the muddy
water of my dream.

---

67. Jung drew the hexagram 50, Ting, the Caldron, describing the *I
Ching* as a caldron, that is a ritual vessel containing spiritual nourishment. "Thus the *I Ching* says of itself I contain (spiritual) nourishment." Jung found himself encouraged to bring it to the attention of
the Western mind. Foreword to the Richard Wilhelm Translation of *I
Ching*, p. xxviii.

The reading of my hexagram showed the way out of winter's stagnation into the fruitful time of summer. It is the last hexagram in the *I Ching*, pointing to the fact that every end contains a new beginning.

> "We shall not cease from exploration
> And the end of all our exploring
> Will be to arrive where we started
> And know the place for the first time."
>
> T.S. Eliot, *Little Gidding*[68]

68. T.S. Eliot, *Four Quartets*, Harcourt, Brace and Company, New York, p. 39. Earlier in the quartet, the same theme is interwoven, "What we call the beginning is often the end/and to make an end is to make a beginning. / The end is where we start from."

12. Trapeze Act

I am on a trapeze with a child balanced on my legs. I am swinging back and forth at the top of a large circus tent.

Then someone else is on the trapeze, and I am down below watching. It is dark inside the tent, except for the spotlight on the trapeze. I see another trapeze artist swinging in the direction of the child and holding a long lance. The person with the child on her legs is no longer moving. A voice from somewhere says, "Hold still." But the other person is coming closer and closer.

I can see the long lance, like a scepter, shining in the light. I see it touch the child who holds still. But the person with the child on her legs moves to make the lance fall. The child loses his balance and falls. It is from very high up. I am shocked and fearful that the child will not survive the fall.

(March 17, 1992)

I have never liked watching trapeze artists at the circus. As a little child at the Barnum and Bailey circus in New York City I used to hide my eyes. It was terrifying to watch the people swinging back and forth on the trapezes. And as a mother, taking our children to the Cirque Knie in Geneva, I still could not watch the trapeze numbers.

Now in my dream, here I was up on the trapeze at the top of the tent. I could feel myself swinging, way up high. Then I was watching from down below, in the dark. I watched in horror as the long lance came closer and closer and finally touched the child, who fell, who was falling when I woke up. I wanted the child to survive.

My dream followed my pilgrimage to the Monastery of Einsiedeln, in the Finsterwald, the dark forest, south of Zurich, where there is the legendary Black Madonna. The founder of the monastery, St. Meinrad, withdrew from his Benedictine Abbey in 822, to live as a hermit in the Finsterwald. He took with him a statue of the Blessed Virgin and built a small sanctuary which he dedicated to the Mother of God.

Upon this site stands the Monastery of Einsiedeln. Over the centuries the statue darkened and the legend of the Black Madonna grew, bringing more and more pilgrims to her side, pilgrims looking for the darker, more feminine side of God.

I too had gone to Einsiedeln as a pilgrim, wanting to visit the shrine of the Black Madonna. I had read many books introducing the mother goddess, excellent books by Harding, Perera, Bolen, Murdock, Woodman. It was time for me to go find her, there where centuries of pilgrimages had darkened her face and hands.

When as an adult, I was welcomed into the Catholic church by a Dominican priest, I chose to add the name of Mary to my name Susan. I wanted consciously to open my heart to the Mother of God, who was hidden away in the Protestant church of my youth. I chose also to enter the church on her feast day, celebrating her Assumption, August 15.[69]

69. This date acquired added significance for me when I learned to appreciate the importance of this "partial recognition of the Mother of God."*Memories, Dreams, Reflections by C.G. Jung*, pp. 227-228, writing about the dogma of the Assumption, pronounced by the Catholic Church in 1950.

However in *Answer to Job*, Jung wrote, "Yahweh's perfectionism is carried over from the Old Testament into the New, and despite all the recognition and glorification of the feminine principle, this never prevailed against the patriarchal supremacy. We have not, therefore, by any means heard the last of it." C.G. Jung, *Answer to Job*, Coll. Works, Vol. 11 (*Jung*, Campbell, p. 566).

I wanted now to go still further and draw close to her dark side, the side of her which was not depicted in the white and blue cherubic statues.

As I walked into the immense baroque church of the ancient Benedictine Abbey, recently restored, I felt overcome with waves of nausea. The walls, the columns, the front altar resembled a giant coral-colored wedding cake, decorated with swirls and gobs of stucco. I wanted to turn around and leave.

Then I saw the small chapel near the main doors, in the middle of the immense nave, facing west. I went and stood in front of this sanctuary. Inside, all was gold, the small altar, the candelabras, the tabernacle, and higher the statue of the Madonna dressed in a gilded sumptuous robe, the Christ Child also crowned and dressed in silk brocade, the hangings, so many clouds and flames and arrows, all in gold. But underneath, the Madonna and the Child were black.

I knelt down and closed my eyes to everything but the blackness. I entered it. Nothing else mattered. It was like a crack, opening into something deeper than anything I had experienced. It was the black tunnel of my childhood nightmares, but it went beyond, with an incredible feeling of both fullness and emptiness at the same time. I was without words, without thoughts. I just was. How long did I remain there immobile? I do not know.

A procession of Benedictine monks came forth from the other side of the chapel, fifty, sixty monks dressed in black robes, carrying the Holy Sacrament. They stopped in front of the sanctuary. I saw their black robes, the round white Blessed Sacrament, and still higher the Black Madonna. Strong deep voices intoned the Salve Regina, "Hail, Holy Queen, mother of mercy."

Why was I so silenced? The monks were quiet and then

went away. I stayed, staring into the darkness, into the unknown, drawn into the abysmal, the void. Falling downward, I had no thoughts, no requests, no prayers. Surrounded by other pilgrims, I would have lain down on the stone floor, with my head in my hands, had there been room.

Where had her blackness come from? The memory of older pagan statues of the Great Goddess?[70] The many fires which destroyed the sanctuary? The smoke of thousands upon thousands of candles, burning day and night in front of her? Or did it come from her compassion, her maternal instinct, which suffers and permits suffering?

Over the centuries, the growing community of monks and pilgrims related more and more deeply to this dark side of the Mother of God which gave also a more human aspect to the Divine Child. And in the early 1800's, when the statue was returned from its safe keeping in Austria during the Napoleon conquests, the community was given the choice to restore the statue to its original whiteness. Of common accord, they chose to keep her black.

Fred Gustafson writes in his book, *The Black Madonna*, that because she is black, she blesses our despair. "As a manifestation of the dark side of life and the psyche, she blesses our pain and suffering as elements in the harmonious balance required if life is to have not only depth

70. "In addition at the time of the Crusades, original pagan images were brought back from the East by returning warriors, as Madonnas... They [the Black Virgins in Europe] would thus be a survival and a continuation under a new name and a new religion of goddesses from the classical world. Ean Begg, *The Cult of the Black Virgin*, Arkana, Penguin Group, London, 1985, pp. 49-50.

M.L. von Franz wrote that the Black Madonna in Einsiedeln "is black because she is more potent and magical and effective than she would be as an ordinary white woman. Here the archetype of the Great Mother Earth comes in through the back door." von Franz, *Shadow and Evil in Fairy Tales*, p. 105.

and continuity, but also hope and promise."[71] Like the
Shulamite who seeks out her groom, the Black Madonna
seeks us out to lead us to wholeness.

> "I am black but beautiful, daughters of Jerusalem,
> like the tents of Kedar,
> like the pavilions of Salmah.
> Take no notice of my swarthiness,
> it is the sun that has burnt me."
>
> The Bride, Song of Songs, 1:5-6[72]

I returned to Geneva the next day, still reeling in the
darkness as the train carried me down the mountains to
the lakeside. My daughter Lucie was waiting for me at the
railroad station.

"Are you all right?" she asked. "You look different.
What happened?"

"The train, tumbling down through the mountains and
the hills to the lake. It was extraordinary."

Lucie took me by the arm. "You know," she said, "if it
makes you feel so good, you could take a train ride each
day."

Was I ready? Not to take a train ride each day, but a soul
ride?

It was that night that I dreamed about the trapeze artist,
high above my head, swinging back and forth, with the
child between her feet.

71. Fred Gustafson, *The Black Madonna*, Sigo Press, Boston, 1990,
p. 103. "The Black Madonna of Einsiedeln is a compensatory psychic
figure. She is an expression of the need for psychic-spiritual wholeness
in an age and culture that has far overvalued the place of reason and
the need for causal explanation. She is the result of this one-sidedness
and serves to bridge the gap. Because of her darkness, she is able to
relate the dark side of the psyche to wholeness." p. 116.
72. The Shulamite woman is the bride in the Song of Songs. "The
blackness of guilt has covered the bridal earth as with black paint. The
Shulamite comes into the same category as those black goddesses (Isis,
Artemis, Parvati, Mary) whose names mean "earth." C.G. Jung, Coll.
Works XIV, p. 420 (Gustafson, p. 101).

Two days later, when I went to see Keller, I lost my way. I was driving to his office, just the other side of the lake, where I'd been going every Wednesday since September. But this time I looked around me and had no idea where I was. The lake was nowhere in sight. Only the road signs pulled me back and pointed me in the right direction.

As Keller opened the door, he looked at me and caught my confusion. He stood back and said nothing. I walked into his office, holding on to my bearings with my eyes. I didn't know where to start. I told him I was lost. He agreed.

Then I told him about going to Einsiedeln and out of the blue or of the dark, I remembered the rat in the train. Between Zurich and the village of Einsiedeln, I had taken a small mountain train, a few wagons with wooden benches. I was looking out the window when a young woman got on and started to settle on the wooden bench opposite me. She looked like one of my daughters in her hippie period, dressed in purple shawls, long beaded earrings, woolen gloves with the tips of the fingers open.

She put down on the bench a string bag which held a baguette, a couples of oranges, a book, and with her other hand, she lowered something else on to the bench before sitting down. I looked closely. It was furry, three colors, white, brown and black, and it had a long, ugly black tail.

"Is that a rat?" I asked, speaking English without thinking.

"Yes," she answered. "It is my rat."

"Do you always travel with it?"

"Yes, it is very intelligent. You are not afraid of it, that is why it is not hiding. It senses right away if someone is afraid or if there is any danger."

I maybe wasn't really afraid of it, but I was certainly surprised. She sat down and shared her sandwich with it, letting it nibble on the cheese. I looked back out the window. I wondered about her English, what was she doing near Einsiedeln?

"Are you living in this area?"

"Yes, my mother is from New Zealand, she married a Swiss carpenter. I was born here."

The train slowed down and she hurriedly reached for her things.

"What is the rat's name?"

She said something that sounded like *No-po*. I asked her what that meant. She said it was Maori and meant from the underworld.

All this I told to Keller.

He sat back delighted. The rat was an image of the night, hungry and instinctual, symbolizing the obscure and unfamiliar side of existence. He was especially delighted with the rat's name. This seemed highly propitious to herald my pilgrimage to the Black Madonna.

He listened as I related my visit, taking myself back to the church, on my knees in front of the sanctuary. I explained how I fell into silence, looking only at the blackness of the statue and disappearing into its darkness. Then the long procession of the black robed monks, the Holy Sacrament held high above their heads, and still higher the Black Madonna. The chanting of Salve Regina.

He talked about the setting, the dark forest – the *Finsterwald* – and how the forest is often the starting point for journeys into the unconscious and an encounter with life and death.[73] It was here that St. Meinrad found shelter and built his sanctuary, placing his statue of the Madonna at the center of his hermitage. Over the centuries, as the Mother of God took on more blackness, the

---

73. According to C.G. Jung, "The forest, dark and impenetrable to the eye like deep water and sea, is the container of the unknown and the mysterious. It is an appropriate synonym for the unconscious." C.G. Jung, Coll. Works XIII, p. 194 (Gustafson, p. 7).

forest became less dark. And Mary became the starting
point for journeys into our depths.

This was what I had experienced. I had entered into my
own inner darkness and was still spiraling downwards on
my way home the next day.

I went on to tell him about my dream that same night.

Swinging on the trapeze with my child on my legs, then
watching from below, seeing the lance approach the
child, the warning "Hold still," the lance falls, the child
falls.

It was one of those sessions where time moves slowly. I
told the dream in French, translating from my notes, and
at the same time reliving it in the language we used
together. This did not restrict or limit me, instead each
week when I re-entered a dream, in another language, it
gave the dream still more breadth.

I told Keller that I did not like watching the trapeze, so
high up in the tent, how I had never liked watching
trapeze artists. How I would always look away. This time I
had not looked away. I had watched the lance come closer
and closer, shining in the light.

"What did you see?" he asked.

"I saw that I was flying too high and couldn't hold still.
I saw the child fall."

"Where were you?"

"I was both below watching and above flying."

"The child could be your spirituality. This would correspond to the symbol of the lance which often carries a
meaning of spiritual discernment."

"And so the dream gives me an image of my spirituality," I said. "It brings me back down from the visit to
Einsiedeln."

"Yes, maybe the altitude was too much. That's what the
rat was warning you. Don't go flying away."

"I should stay closer to the ground?"

"Yes, closer to your instincts."

It was time to leave. I was still dizzy – full of my trapeze dream and of the Black Madonna.

Back home, when I was sitting at my desk, I felt a sore spot on my chest. I had all but forgotten the morning's visit to the doctor and the resulting small operation. I had checked with my dermatologist about a mole on my breast, and he had decided to cut it out right there and then.

The doctor's scalpel had cut deep right above my heart, there where I was still suntanned from years of swimming and life-guarding at the village pool in Briarcliff. He had sewn ten stitches. Now, the incision was beginning to burn. I could still hear the knife cutting around the mole and see the doctor's hand. He had said he would have the laboratory results in five days. My father had died of a skin cancer on his chest. It had turned into a malignant melanoma before he had shown it to the doctor.

That night I slept very little. Pierre was traveling. Most every week during the entire year, Pierre worked a few days at his company's office in southern France. I had not told him about the visit to the doctor. Being alone so much of the time had let me enter more deeply into my analysis, my dreams, my inward seeking.

I lay still on my bed and felt pinned down by the scalpel. I realized I was grounded. I was no longer flying. And inside me there was darkness. "Salve Regina, mater misericordiae…" Some of the words came back in Latin, an echo of the years when it was part of our evening prayer, when as a young couple we belonged to a lay movement of spirituality. I prayed to the Black Madonna. Mother of Mercy. There was a dark side. There was suffering and death. "Mary, Mother of God," I prayed, "show me the way to both life and death."

The fires that had burned down the sanctuary, the candles that had darkened its walls, all this I felt. I was again on my knees in front of the Madonna's blackened face. The night surrounded me. There was a cycle of birth, life, and death. I was part of it. This was my cycle.

The next few days I kept to my room. The pain became less severe. I rested and read. But when I walked around, I felt nauseous and dizzy. Pierre returned on Friday. He listened, concerned about the operation, trying to understand where it had taken me. By Sunday I was feeling better and could move about normally.

Monday I called the doctor. The report was negative. He was very matter-of-fact about the whole thing. He said he would take out the stitches at the end of the week.

The following Wednesday when I returned to Keller, I spoke of this operation done a week ago, on that same day when I had gotten lost driving to his office, and of the pain that night. I told him about the mole and my father's cancer. The doctor's scalpel and the burning incision. How I lay on my bed, grounded.

"Yes, you were grounded, no longer flying on your trapeze. But there is more. There is the cancer of your father, the cancer which killed him. What do you remember of this?"

I told him about the last visit I had with my father, a few weeks before his death, how he sat on the shaded porch with the heating pad on his chest where the tumor was.

"It is this cancer which you have just cut out."

He went on to explain. Each of us sees our identity through the image which our parents have of us. The father looks to his daughter for the feminine aspects which he needs. This image is like a stigma on the daughter's breast. The scalpel cut out the mole, cut out the stigma, the image my father had of me, the image that the patriarchy bestows on its daughters. Now the father's phallic paradigms fall away.

Paradigms. I thought of competition, success, power, control, determination, the code of behavior I had accepted and lived by for over fifty years.

"This projection of the father's anima placed you too high, in the air, too far from the ground."

I was deeply stirred by this. I was flying too high and was now back down on the ground.

"This does not mean that your drive for excellency will disappear, but it will be less active. You can sit back and be still."

With relief I welcomed his words. I can be still.

It fit together. The Black Madonna was showing me the way.

Because of her darkness, she could lead me through my own darkness to my soul.[74]

> "Return, return, O maid of Shulam,
> Return, return, that we may gaze on you!"
>
> The Song of Songs, 7,1 (The Chorus)

---

74. "She [the Black Virgin] takes the feminine into the core (Kore) of her own matter (mother) where she can never doubt the presence of her own soul resonating in her own body." Marion Woodman, *Leaving My Father's House*, p. 113.

The Black Madonna and Child are clothed in gold.
(Benedictine Abbey, Einsiedeln, Switzerland)

13. Vertigo

There are orange and red flames rising from a small
fire, dark branches of wood are burning. A large white
bird comes close to the flames. The bird has powerful
wings, which are wide open. It catches fire, turns brilliant
red, and disappears in the flames, sending sparks of fire
into the air.

(April 12, 1992)

This was an afternoon dream, after a morning of skiing
in the Swiss Alps where I was laid low with vertigo. When
I finally reached home, my Swedish friend Kim was waiting for me, coming to stay for a short visit. But I was still
so shaken and dizzy that I went first to my room to rest a
moment. I woke up with this image of a white bird, big
like an eagle, caught in the middle of flames.

I put my dream aside and went for a walk with Kim. I
shared with her my experience of vertigo. I told her how
even the drive up to the ski resort had tormented me,
making me close my eyes and not look at the mountain
scenery.

I explained how more and more I felt physically ill
when I was close to the Alps. At first, arriving from New
York, studying in Grenoble, I had loved the high mountains. Every street in the city seemed to end in a mountain. I wanted to go up into them. I learned to follow
Pierre down the ski trails. We hiked and climbed over the
mountain passes. I met his family at their chalet in
Samoëns, a small village in Haute Savoie. We vacationed

there every winter and summer, first the two of us, and then with our children. We skied in wintertime and hiked in summertime. We stayed overnight in refuges high in the mountains, all together.

But then as I grew older, the mountains started to oppress me. I no longer wanted to climb up the trails, ski down the slopes. I no longer wanted to feel them towering over me. I didn't want to look at them. When I returned to Samoëns, staying in my family-in-law's chalet, I'd turn my eyes away from the heights. And when I'd try to go along with Pierre up the slopes, it became more and more difficult. I was pitting my will power against something stronger than myself.

Then there was this last weekend. We were invited to stay with friends. Saturday, the drive up the mountainside had made me feel so nauseous that I did not go skiing and stayed inside the rest of the day, not wanting to even go for a walk. However, Sunday morning, our friends were exhausted, and Pierre had no one to ski with. I finally said I would go with him.

We took a first chairlift, and immediately I became dizzy. I couldn't look down, the height petrified me, nor could I look up for the sheer mountain tops closed in on me. My head throbbed. Pierre told me there were two more chairlifts ahead of us. I continued to follow. The mountains got steeper and steeper. Soon there were no more trees, only jagged rock cliffs and crests of snow and ice. I closed my eyes and saw all red, then I saw all black. I told Pierre that I felt awful, but I couldn't turn back. The trail we were to ski down started at the top and went down far from where we were.

We skied to the second chairlift. I again closed my eyes, to try to quiet my nausea. I was going upwards, but it felt like I was sinking. I opened my eyes, there were chairlifts going in every direction, all in black and white, twisted cables, crisscrossed metal pylons, sheer rock, ice, as if there had been a cataclysm and the side of the dark mountain had erupted. I shut tight my eyes until the end of the ride.

Still another short descent to the third lift, the noise of the skis and skiboards was magnified tenfold. People raced past, going too fast, colliding, crashing into snow banks. I wanted to scream but it was too much of an effort. I pushed myself into the last chairlift and tried to think about breathing slowly, evenly. The sun was hot on my face. Every part of my body hurt.

We were at the top of the trail. Pierre suggested we rest, take a cup of tea on the terrace of the refuge which hung over the cliff. He wanted so much for me to feel better, to enjoy the altitude, the snow, the sun. I knew I couldn't. I was incapable of taking my skis off, and still more incapable of walking. I wanted only to lie down, but there was no place, not one square meter of flat space. Instead I leaned against Pierre, gathering what strength I could.

We started down. I held my eyes on the few meters ahead of me. Only the desire to get off the blasted mountain kept me going. Constantly I felt pulled to the side which dropped off into empty space. I fought it, hugging the other side. I started crying. We were only half way. The tears froze around my eyes, but I continued, fearing if I stopped, I'd feel worse. Pierre skied slowly ahead of me, showing me the way, waiting for me. I followed frozen with fear, like a block of ice. I hated it. I hated every bit of it. I hated all the other times I had skied. I hated every mountain in France. I hated every mountain in Switzerland.

We hit the tree level and I realized that soon I'd be down. My whole body ached. When at last I arrived at the bottom, I started trembling. Without taking my skis off, I lay down on a large rock, closed my eyes, and sobbed.

I didn't tell Kim all this, only enough so she could somehow understand my anguish. As we walked I started to feel better. We walked for a long time, down the road opposite our house. The blossoms, the forsythia, the Japanese cherry trees, all the flowers were palpably beautiful, the colors so intense I could feel them. As I stared at them, I wanted to pull them close to me, to become part of them. I was a little afraid, I felt awake to something new, and unfamiliar with the intensity of what I was experiencing. When we arrived back at the house, Pierre was working at his desk and called to us from his upstairs window. I remember not being able to look up.

Kim stayed overnight. I carried on like my normal self but I wasn't. It was as if a part of me was moving around, but the underneath part of me was elsewhere. After she left, I slept. I was seized with exhaustion. I saw again the white bird of my dream and decided to try to draw it. It's head was looking up, the wide wings were spread open, below it were flames from a small fire.

In drawing it, I wondered if it might be a phoenix, but I wasn't sure what a phoenix looked like. The bird I had drawn was big like an eagle. I went to look up phoenix in the encyclopedia and there on the page was exactly the bird I had drawn, the bird of my vision. The head, wings and flames were identical. I read how this mythological bird, every 500 years, burned itself on a funeral pyre and how another phoenix arose from the ashes with renewed youth and beauty. Even the branches and the flames looked like those I had drawn.

A phoenix.

I turned to my book on symbols. My bird was a symbol of immortality and rebirth. "The phoenix which rises from the ashes of the fire is the symbol of the phenomenon which manifests itself when life is at its most bleak, then something unexpected emerges to fill the vacuum.

This is the opportunity for fresh life and inspiration to surge up from within."[75]

And I had dreamed of a phoenix after my vertigo.

All this seemed important, but what took my breath away was the picture in the encyclopedia. Again I had seen something in a dream which I consciously could not identify. Not until I looked it up, was I aware that the bird in the middle of the flames was a phoenix, resembling exactly the bird pictured on the page of the encyclopedia.

Wednesday when I saw Keller, I said the week had been difficult. Then I laughed, as if to brush away the importance I was giving to my own experience and emotions. I sat still a few minutes and then told him first about the mountains, my vertigo, closing my eyes, the anguish, always higher. I was speaking more quickly. The bare mountain, the bright sun, the rocky ledges, the ice, the tangle of cables, the chaos. And then the descent, the vertigo and waves of nausea, my tears, and finally the earth, lying down on the rock.

Keller was quiet. He looked at me and said, "You were right not to want to go to the mountains, and still less to go up to the top. It is not the place for someone awakening to the unconscious. Instead you wanted to stay close to the earth, in the shade, in the dark."

He was rather alarmed, suggesting that I had put myself into a dangerous situation and that my body had reacted. I was nauseous and dizzy, and still I went ever higher into the brilliant sun.

75. Tom Chetwynd, *A Dictionary of Symbols*, Grafton Books, London, 1982, p. 52. "The phoenix was identified as the dawn sun, rising brilliantly through the grayness of the first light: which is an allusion to the continuity of life, through cycles of change and transformation." p. 52 "As a symbol of origins, the phoenix is also a symbol of rebirth. He is consumed in the very fire which he brought, i.e. the fire of life gives birth and destroys." p. 307.

"You were literally tearing yourself apart. You wanted to go down, this is yin. Instead you were going up, this is yang. The double movement paralyzed you."

Yin, yang. The two parts of the circle in early Chinese philosophy, the light and the dark. The yang actually means "banners waving in the sun," and the yin means "the cloudy, the overcast." The banners waving in the sun are the snow covered mountain tops, and the cloudy, the overcast, shades the earth below.[76]

"You should have gone to the seaside, to water, to mist and fog. You closed your eyes in order to go there within yourself."

With centuries, yang came to represent the sun, the strong, the firm, hence the masculine. And yin to represent the moon, the receptive, the yielding, hence the feminine.

"You closed your eyes to the yang images in order to find something more maternal. The cliffs, the metal cables, the ice, the brilliant sun, these are all hard, masculine images. And so you suffered vertigo, the attraction of what is below, the attraction of yin."

This spoke very true. Even sitting there in his office, I wanted to close my eyes and sink into the chair. In a way disappear downwards. What was this yin pull, this movement into darkness?

76. "East and West are two halves of a whole; they represent the two inner aspects of each individual man and woman. The psychological split needs healing through an inner union, allowing for between left and right hemispheres, between scientific and spiritual, masculine and feminine, yin and yang." Jean Shinoda Bolen, *Tao of Psychology*, p. 9.

When there is this inner union, there is the experience of the Tao, represented in the image of the circle divided with a slanting S line. On one side light, yang; on the other side dark, yin. "The idea of the circle is ancient, but the symbol divided into black and white dates from tenth-century neo-Confucianism." *Tao Te Ching*, Lao Tsu, Translated by Gia-Fu Feng & Jane English, Introduction by Jacob Needleman, Vintage Books, 1989, p. xxii.

"It's the dialectic of the psyche. When the life of the psyche goes too far in one direction, then it comes back in the other direction. It is like the pendulum on a clock, swinging back and forth. We have to accept this movement."[77]

I had been in the sun on top of the mountains long enough. It was time for me to go into the dark, down in the valley. I had lived very consciously, now it was time to live unconsciously.

Keller insisted. "But be careful. The encounter with the unconscious is an encounter with fire."

Fire.

Flames.

The phoenix. I related the vision I had of the white bird in the middle of flames, of my drawing, and the realization that it was a phoenix. How taken aback I was to find the same drawing in the encyclopedia.

"The phoenix is a powerful image," Keller said, "it can be burned and reborn. Something has been burned away."

I told Keller that the burning of the bird, the reddening, had spoken to me of what I had been reading and rereading in Marie-Louise von Franz' book, *Alchemy*. It had happened after my vertigo in the mountains. There had been something similar to *nigredo*, a darkening, on my way up the slope, and then a whitening, an *albedo* on my way down.

---

77. Jung borrowed the term enantiodromia from Heraclitus, meaning that one extreme will inevitably turn into or elicit its opposite. "Applied to both personal and collective life, it suggests that the pendulum swing between extremes tends toward a more humane and inclusive centeredness capable of relating to, even appreciating, extremes without identifying with them." John Dourley, *The Illness That We Are*, Inner City Books, Toronto, 1984, p. 28.

"This is very powerful," he said. "The double movement, yin and yang, has brought on the phoenix. Something new is being born. Don't try to hold on to the ashes."

We remained with von Franz and my feelings about discovering the *rubedo* in the burning phoenix. Yes, after the reddening, a new awareness. I was to let go of my old consciousness.

"It's time to live in this new state of awareness with a consciousness that doesn't want anything more."

I drove home feeling very much alive. The fire was still smoldering. Instead of writing down my thoughts like I usually do after each session, I went for a walk, back down the road where I walked with Kim a few days earlier. I returned to where I had looked at the wild cherry blossoms, where I had felt the pink, the color pink, so intensely. I returned to the blossom. The branch looked maimed and mutilated, there where the bud was bursting forth. The blackness of the bark was burned open. The flower was being born.

Birth. Death. Rebirth.

Back home, at my desk, as I opened my journal and started to write about the birth of the cherry flower, I stopped in wonder. My last journal entry, written earlier that same morning, spoke of the birth of another flower.

"April 15: My first granddaughter is born.

Her name is Flora."

14. Bird-Women

I follow my friend Kim across some fields and into an old Mexican church. Several people are already seated. I take a chair and sit at the right end of the first row. Kim sits in the middle. The church fills up and becomes like a huge tent. I wait quietly and pray.

Then many large, earthly women, wearing masks with beaked noses, come on the stage in front of me. They wear loose-sleeved blouses and long skirts in bright blues, reds, and yellows. They are dancing to primitive music, seeming to chase invisible spirits.

Next come enormous animals, ones I've never seen before, coming from the middle of the stage, swaying and walking down the aisle, next to me. A very large one, like a rhinoceros, moves close to me and brushes my side.

The entire setting – the tent, the stage, the audience – is very primitive, full of power, but not frightening. I know there will be more scenes.

(April 24, 1992)

It was the morning alarm which woke me. I wanted to go back to the dream to see the next scenes. For a little while, I was back in the church tent. There were still more large animals, lumbering down the aisle. But then I woke up again. Later during the day, when I would bring the dream back, I could still see the animals and I especially saw the bird-women with their brightly colored skirts, swaying back and forth on the stage.

The vision of these women awakened my senses, making my skin tingle. I felt enkindled, almost eroticized. I liked carrying this image around with me. I liked imagining myself sitting there in the tent. I closed my eyes and I saw again those magnificent women, winding their way on the stage, going swish with their sleeves and skirts.

Still today, I hold on to this dream like I would a painting. In this way it remains alive. I remember James Hillman suggesting that instead of rationally interpreting a dream, we befriend it, we become familiar with it, taking time to listen to it, like in a friendship.[78] In other words, instead of bringing the dream up to me, I go down to it, or at least I meet it halfway.

I befriended my bird-women. I joined them, putting on a brightly colored long skirt. And I danced with them in the church.

Prior to this dream, many months earlier, in the beginning of my analysis, I had dreamed of another church, one here in Geneva. I was going into the side chapel for morning Mass.

It is a weekday in the morning. Many women are already in the chapel. I go in and sit down. There is a new priest. I close my eyes and try to pray. The priest is asking questions, we are supposed to answer from the papers on our chairs. I keep my eyes closed and don't read the papers. I want to shut out the noise and pray. I am afraid he will ask me something.

It is time to stand if I want to take communion. I open my eyes. Instead of communion, refreshments are going to be served. The priest is still talking. The women are

---

78. "For a dream image to work in life it must, like a mystery, be experienced as fully real. Interpretation arises when we have lost touch with the images." James Hillman, *The Dream and the Underworld*, p. 123.

now moving about. They have set up large counters in the
middle of the chapel, with snacks and drinks.

I realize I can hardly breathe. I can not get a deep
breath. I rush outside for air.

(October 1, 1991)

Instead of setting me afire, this early dream in my
analysis had suffocated me. I had to run outside for fresh
air. When I spoke of it to Keller, it brought laughter to my
lips. It was humorous, opening my eyes for the Eucharist
and seeing a refreshment counter instead of the altar.

Keller had reminded me that breath is the age-old
symbol of life and spirit. "Yahweh God fashioned man of
dust from the soil. He breathed into his nostrils a breath
of life, and the man became a living being." (Genesis 2,7)

The breath of the Lord is the gift of the Holy Spirit.[79]
Without the Spirit, the house of the Lord was without air,
without life, and I was suffocating.

In my dream I had entered the chapel to attend Mass,
to participate in the mystery of the Eucharist. But instead
of a meaningful liturgy, people were talking, the priest
was asking questions, and there were papers to read.
Activity had replaced ritual.[80] The life of spirit was being
snuffed out.

I had been drawn to the Catholic Church through the
liturgy of the Eucharist, which I saw as the symbol of

79. "The Hebrew word for breath, *ruah*, is translated by Spirit, corresponding to the Greek word *pneuma* and the Latin *spiritus. Ruah,
pneuma, spiritus* signify the breath which comes out of the nose and
mouth. This breath has a mysterious action and is compared to wind."
Dictionnaire des Symboles, edited by Robert Laffont, Paris, 1982, p. 900.
80. In an essay on Ritual Process, Initiation, and Contemporary Religion, Robert Moore underlines "the continuing human need for the
experience of transformative ritual." He sees ritual as a process of
constructing a "space/time pod" necessary for personal and social
growth. Stein & Moore, *Jung's Challenge to Contemporary Religion*,
pp. 147-155.

God's incarnation. Over the years, I continued to be nourished by the symbolism of the Eucharist. As we moved around Europe, we structured the life of our family around the liturgical calendar and participated in the life of the local parish. There were long periods when I went to daily Mass, and often I went away on retreats of silence and prayer.

I needed this time away from the needs of family, of friends and of community – the school committees, the church committees, the social and political commitments. I needed this time alone to find myself. Where was my home? What was my language? Why was I living here in Europe? Who was I deep down? Joseph Campbell would have said, "Where was my bliss?"

These were the questions that led me to writing. I discovered that if I wrote honestly, it was a way of learning who I was. If I wrote about making houses into homes, I would discover the part of me that was Hestia. Was I chained to the hearth or did the hearth give me meaning and set me free? I could understand my feelings of frustration when time after time people asked if I worked or if I stayed at home.

If I wrote about life, I would discover its cycles, life, death and rebirth. I would say good-bye to my grandmother the way I had instinctively wanted to, in her coffin in our living room, releasing her in my memory. And I could come to grips with my father's struggle with cancer, finding a metaphor for his powerlessness, a metaphor that would remind me of mine.

It was about this time that our local priest, Father Richard Frost, gave a series of talks on C.G. Jung and spirituality. I read Jung's *Answer to Job*. Here I saw Job's confrontation with God as revelatory of a creature who was part of his Creator, becoming conscious of the oneness of all creation. "God is Reality itself and therefore –

last but not least – man."[81] It was lightning. Questions which I had buried were answered. God, love, creation, the ocean of the collective unconscious, all spoke of the same source.

My faith emerged from a long chrysalis, more vibrant than before. With enthusiasm I turned to Jung's autobiography, *Memories, Dreams, Reflections by C.G. Jung,* recorded by Aniela Jaffé at the end of his life. I read *Man And His Symbols,* in which Jung and his co-writers examine the world of the unconscious as revealed through symbols. I plunged into mythology, reading and rereading Edith Hamilton's *Mythology* until the gods and heroes came to life in my imagination. I read *Myths to Live by,* and other works of Joseph Campbell, letting mythology draw me to the "mind at large." I read more and more of Jung and of Jungian thinking. And I went back to Saint Teresa, Thomas Merton, Teilhard de Chardin. I continued writing in my journal and began writing down my dreams. I wanted to bring my mind and my soul together. I was ready to take the next step which for me was a Jungian analysis.

This is where I was, a few months later, when I dreamed about the chapel here in Geneva. I had gone there for Mass, for the liturgy of the Eucharist which was again

81. C.G. Jung, *The Answer to Job,* Coll. Works, Vol. 11 (*Jung,* Campbell, p. 569). "Loudly as Yahweh's power resounds through the universe, the basis of its existence is correspondingly slender, for it needs conscious reflection in order to exist in reality. Existence is only real when it is conscious to somebody. That is why the Creator needs conscious man." p. 535.

The theme that God needs man in order to become conscious of His whole self is developed in Edward Edinger's *The Creation of Consciousness,* Inner City Books, Toronto, 1984. "On the basis of our emerging knowledge of the unconscious, the traditional image of God has been enlarged. Traditionally God has been pictured as all-powerful and all-knowing ... The extent of divine *awareness* did not receive much attention ... His omnipotence omniscience and divine purpose are not always *known* to him. He needs man's capacity to know Him in order to know Himself." p. 23.

strongly nourishing my faith. In this mystery, I saw humanity – my humanity, my humanness – imaged in the bread, as being transformed little by little into divinity. Jung saw here the soul finding its wholeness, "the rite of individuation."[82] But instead of mystery and transformation, there was in my dream noise and confusion. I lost my breath and rushed outdoors for air.

Six months later, I dreamed of a different church. It was a Mexican church, like the white adobe chapels Pierre and I had visited in New Mexico, near Taos, full of color, open spaces, painted clay statues of saints and animals and plants. There was one special sanctuary at Chimaya where I found healing earth in a small pit in the sacristy. I brought some of this earth back with me to Geneva. It was time to turn to it.

In my dream, the church became a round tent with bird-women in bright colors dancing on the stage, long skirts swishing back and forth, and animals, immense beasts careening down the aisles, brushing against me. I was not suffocating. On the contrary I was exhilarated. I was filled with new life, I was filled with the spirit.

By Wednesday when I went to see Keller, the dream was haunting me. I was identifying with the bird-women. I was going swish to the spirits. Keller gave me a second sideways glance, and said nothing. I was on stage, in a brightly colored skirt, with a mask and a beaked nose. My dream spilled over into his office.

---

82. John P. Dourley, *The Illness That We Are*, p. 52. The author, Catholic priest and Jungian analyst, cites here Jung's essay on transformation symbolism in the Mass: "The mystery of the Eucharist transforms the soul of the empirical man, who is only part of himself, into his totality, symbolically expressed by Christ. In this sense, therefore, we can speak of the rite of the individuation process." CW 11, par.414.

Dourley continues, "Through the re-enactment of the central events in the myth of Christ – here understood as a figure representing universal humanity – the ego (Son, Christ) is sacrificed to the unconscious (Father) to rise again in the experience of Spirit-Self." pp. 52-53.

"This is true religion," he said. "Not the Catholic religion nor the Protestant nor any other doctrinal religion. This is instinctive religion. Mexico, women disguised as birds with enormous beaks, the colors, the music, the animals, the sensuality, everything is there. This is not a religion of the mind, it is a religion of the whole being."

Keller seemed to see the women and the animals like I did. I felt myself swaying.

"True religion," he continued, "has an ecstatic quality. It can carry us beyond our reason into a mystical spell. You understand, our consciousness is very partial. When we experience an emotion which transports us, we are given a glimpse into the depth and the immensity of our unconsciousness."

Ecstasy. I repeated the word. I thought of Dionysus, the god of wine and ecstasy[83]. I felt again the intensity of the colors, the sounds, the movements. This was far away from the annoying activity in the morning chapel of my earlier dream.

Keller repeated, "This is instinctive religion, involving all your senses."

My senses. Sensation, that fourth function, which according to Jungian psychology is one of the irrational aspects of our personality. Jung defined four functions, set in two opposing pairs. The first pair is rational: thinking and feeling (feeling something is right or wrong). The second pair is irrational: intuiting and sensing. Jung believed that each of us specializes in one function which he named our "superior" function, and overlooks the other one of the same pair, our "inferior" function.

---

83. "Ecstasy – the Dionysian experience – may be intellectually unfamiliar. But in ecstatic expression we will recognize a long forgotten part of ourselves that makes us truly alive and connects us with every living thing. In Greek myth that part of ourselves is represented by Dionysus." Robert Johnson, *Ecstasy*, Harper, San Francisco, 1987, p. 3.

I had tried to understand these functions, starting with another more basic Jungian differentiation: extravert or introvert.[84] I speculated that I was both, with a slight preference for introversion, for solitary dreaming to group acting. As for the four functions, I felt quite sure that I was mostly intuitive, if I gave myself a chance. I felt also quite sure that sensing, perceiving through the senses, was low on the list.

Then in our workshop, one of our writers who is a Myers-Briggs consultant, gave us our type indicators. We were all more intuitive and feeling, than sensing and thinking. This she felt could be expected for writers. We tended to place imagination above concrete detail, and listening to others above logic.

I wondered about this. I wondered about the concrete detail, about my sensations. Could this really be my "inferior" function? Could this function represent an unlived aspect of my life? Were my bird-women leading me somewhere quite different?

"Your bird-women are instinctive," continued Keller, "and they are also spiritual. Birds are spiritual beings, they fly between heaven and earth, symbols of life and immortality."[85]

---

84. Jung first postulated two fundamental attitudes: extraversion (oriented outwards) and introversion (oriented inwards), one of which is prominent in each individual. He then defined the four functions.
"There are four aspects of psychological orientation. In order to orient ourselves, we must have a function which ascertains that something is there (sensation); a second function which establishes what it is (thinking); a third function which states whether it suits us or not (feeling), and a fourth function which indicates where it came from and where it is going (intuition)." C.G. Jung, *Psychology and Religion: West and East*, Coll. Works, Vol. 11, p. 167 (Glossary, *Memories, Dreams Reflections by C.G. Jung*).
85. The flight of birds symbolizes the relationship between heaven and earth. In *Le Dictionnaire des Symboles* bird-men are mentioned and interpreted as shamen, their flight as the ecstatic dance.

I had seen the powerful beaks. Now I saw the colored blouses and skirts as the feathered wings and tails, ready to swirl and fly away.

"The women-birds symbolize the new *coniunctio*, the union of the body and the spirit. This is the essence of religion, this is what the mystics talk about, this is what Saint Teresa was talking about."

Keller looked at me. I returned his look.

We had often talked about Saint Teresa, the book I had read by Welch, *Spiritual Pilgrims*, comparing her spiritual path and Jung's, her writings, *The Interior Castle*, her ecstatic meditations, "a caressing of love so sweet."[86] Again I felt I had gone full circle.

It was time to leave. I was tired. I needed time to rest before I danced again with my bird-women.

"Try to find moments of solitude in the days ahead," Keller said, "and live with an open heart. This is perhaps your spiritual way."

I had time to be alone. Pierre was traveling. I was limiting myself outside the home. I needed the solitude for my dreams and analysis, for my moments of quiet prayer, and for my writing and reflections.

It was spring and I remember feeling – really feeling, physically – the pale white and lilac primroses pierce through the dark grass. From the window near my desk, I watched the forsythia bush slowly turn yellow. I was the alchemist. The branches bent under the weight of their golden flowers.

---

86. "The soul is satisfied now with nothing less than God. The pain is not bodily, but spiritual; though the body has its share in it, even a large one. It is a caressing of love so sweet which now takes place between the soul and God, that I pray God of His goodness to make him experience it who many think that I am lying." Meditation from St. Teresa of Avila (1515-1582), Woodman, *Addiction to Perfection*, p. 183.

Coniunctio. This was the word Keller had used, the concept of Jung that out of the conflict of twoness emerges the third[87]. My dream was like what happens in an alchemist's vessel, sublimating consciousness out of unconsciousness. I saw here again the sacrament of the Eucharist, the *coniunctio* of Creator and creation. The incarnation. God becoming man so that man becomes God. The spirit becoming visible. This was the imagery that had led me to the Catholic faith and that was now showing me a new born world.

I remembered the myth of the White Bison Spirit Woman who visited the Sioux nation, bringing the first sacred medicine pipe to the Oglala people. When she was still far away in the fields, she told a scout that she was coming and that they should build a large tepee for her in the center of their nation. When she arrived, she was very beautiful and she was singing. As she went into the tepee this is what she sang:

"With visible breath I am walking.
A voice I am sending as I walk.
In a sacred manner I am walking.
With visible tracks I am walking.
In a sacred manner I walk."[88]

87. James Hall underlined the importance of observing the gradual appearance of *coniunctio* imagery. "Much of the work of analysis, indeed, seems to be to maintain a steady and reliable containing structure in which preparations for the *coniunctio* can safely take place." Hall, *Jungian Dream Interpretation*, p. 98. See footnote 58, p. 106.

88. "She is not physical; she is Psyche, Pneuma, Light as wind, yet her tracks may be seen. She renders the sacred accessible in the here and now: touched, felt, and experienced as though it were physical. The spirit world is made immediate and palpable through symbolic experience." Robert Johnson, *We*, Harper, San Francisco, 1983, pp. 169-173.

The Spirit Woman came with visible breath, with visible tracks. She came walking in a sacred manner and she entered the large tepee in the middle of the land.

And so with my dream, I was building a tepee in the center of my life, a tent, a sacred circle, where I could dance with my bird women, in loose-sleeved blouses and long dresses of bright blues, reds, and yellows. Where I could dance with visible breath, with visible tracks.

15. Pieces of Gold

It is nighttime. I am going through a moonlit yard, around a large mansion with lights in the windows. I go inside and find myself in a small room with Pierre. We are looking at gold jewelry which is mine or which I am going to acquire. A dark figure is behind us, watching. At first we think he is perhaps there to admire the gold or to sell it. Then we realize that he wants to steal the jewelry.

Pierre leaves me, and I put the pieces safely away. The dark figure is still in the room. I don't recognize him, his face does not stand out, he is young like in his twenties. I go near him and tell him in a low voice to go away.

(May 22, 1992)

I liked the night and the moonlit yard, the mansion with lighted windows, circling and going inside and still further into a smaller room. I liked the gold. It took me back to Marie Louis von Franz's book, *Alchemy*, which I had read and reread during the year, and to Bosnak's little book *Dreams* which uses alchemy as a way to re-enter our dreams.[89]

In alchemical terms, gold is the end product, the result of the many step process of refining base metals. In

---

89. "C.G. Jung turned to alchemy to learn about our world of dream images. As well as being the archaic form of chemistry, alchemy also comprised the study of processes of imagination that took place in connection with the impossible task of transforming base metals into precious metals. This unreachable goal of refining matter through technique, concentration, and God's help aroused the passion of many in medieval times." Robert Bosnak, *A Little Course in Dreams*, pp. 60-73.

Alchemy is a way into dreams and analysis.
(Alchemists at work, 18th century manuscript)

psychological terms, gold is the symbol of the Self, the way of individuation, the contribution of each of us to the collective Self, to God[90]. As alchemists strove to liberate the precious metal within its vessel of matter, so Jung used the symbolism to liberate the Self within the chaos and darkness of the unconscious.

During the year I had worked with the different stages of alchemy in many of the sessions with Keller. They had meaning for me. *Nigredo*, the blackening, the firing and melting out, the initial period of self reflection[91], the darkness of descending into the unknown, losing control, the black swirling waters in my dreams, winter's depression.

Albedo, the whitening, the distilling and the washing, becoming quieter, and more detached and objective[92], bringing the shadow into the light, differentiating the opposites, the attraction of the yin, letting in the unexpected, standing in the stream of water.

And then it started all over, *nigredo, albedo*. Again and again. Each time when I felt I had learned something, I was right back at the beginning. Dejected, laid low by the witch and a *hexenschuss*. Out of breath. Trying to hold on. My ego uncertain about what to do next. Vertigo. My eyes closed. Until I started the whole process once again.

90. "The God-image does not coincide with the unconscious as such, but with a special content of it, namely the archetype of the self... One can then explain the God-image as a reflection of the self, or conversely, explain the self as an *imago Dei* in man." C.G. Jung, *Psychology and Religion, West and East*, Coll. Works, Vol. 11, pp. 468ff, p. 190 (Glossary, *Memories, Dreams, Reflections by C.G. Jung*).
91. "The blackness, the terrible depression and state of dissolution which has to be compensated by the hard work of the alchemist." M.L. von Franz, *Alchemy*, An Introduction to the Symbolism and the Psychology, Inner City Books, Toronto, 1980, p. 220.
92. "Whiteness suggests purification, no longer contaminated with matter, taking back our projections ... the first stage of becoming quieter and more detached." Ibid., p. 222.

When finally, after many repetitions, after returning into the swirling dark water, burning away old attitudes, bathing the inner child, encountering the Black Madonna, there was a little something which held. *Rubedo*, the reddening, the union with the anima,[93] dancing with the bird-women, the moment of rebirth, the phoenix, the light born in the darkness, the *coniunctio*.

So there I was in my dream with a few pieces of gold. I wanted to put them away, hide them from the thief, keep them safe. Who is this dark figure? I tell him to go away, to get out of my moonlit mansion.

But when I took the dream to Keller, he told me that gold cannot be put away. The light that comes into the darkness has to circulate, otherwise it goes out. I thought about the light in the Gospel that is not put under a bowl, but on a lamp-stand so that it can shine, otherwise it is not seen (Luke 8:16).

"Gold comes from the unconscious, from the Self. When it comes into our hands it is true self-esteem, our true self-value," said Keller. "And at the same time gold returns to the unconscious, to the Self."

---

93. Von Franz illustrates this step with the Annunciation, quoting Jung, "Analysis should release an experience that grips or falls upon us as from above, an experience that has substance and body such as those things which occurred to the ancients. If I were going to symbolize it I would choose the Annunciation." Von Franz continues, "In alchemical terms that is the beginning of the rubedo." *Alchemy*, p. 269.

In classical alchemical terms, von Franz names a fourth step, *citrinitas*, the circulation of light, the circulation of the philosopher's stone. It is in the *rubedo/citrinitas* stage, that a new form of consciousness evolves, which von Franz describes as conscious spontaneity: "To climb out of the water and sit in the sun and then have to jump back into the water is a very dangerous business ... The second phase is conscious spontaneity in which the participation of consciousness is not lost and that is something very difficult because it is so much easier to go on overanalyzing or to slip back into the former state of unconsciousness." p. 229.

The dark thief of my dream was right in coming for the gold.

"The unconscious can not be capitalized. The pieces of gold have to return to the collective pool."

Keller suddenly resembled the dark thief. He wasn't going to let me put my pieces of gold in the drawer.

"This thief in your dream is a Hermes-like character, the God of thieves. He threatens to steal the gold. He warns you not to conserve it."

I knew Hermes to be the God of thieves, the Trickster, the God who as a baby, scarcely a few hours old, stole Apollo's cattle. I knew him also to the be the messenger God, the guide of souls.[94] I listened carefully.

"Hermes is the god of movement, of new beginnings."

And so his winged hat and sandals.

"Everything evolves, changes," Keller continued. "An insight which we have today is no longer valid tomorrow. Every truth must give way to a new truth."

I somewhere knew he was right but I felt exhausted.

"With everything constantly changing," I said, "what's left to hold on to?"

"Nothing. Don't hold on, let go."

"Let go also of the gold?"

"Yes, let it circulate. And remember that even speaking about it is a way of trying to hold on to it."

So no more words about gold! I would put my gold aside. No, I would let it flow.

I was soon to go on vacation with Pierre to the Cyclades, some of the Greek islands, and for the rest of the session we talked about Delos, the home of Apollo, the son of Leto and Zeus, and twin brother of Artemis. It seemed

---

94. "Through metaphor, he was the guide of souls on a mystical and psychological journey that sought to unite male and female elements." Jean Shinoda Bolen, *Gods in Everyman*, Harper and Row, New York, 1989, p. 166.

right that I had not yet visited these islands. I had not yet
related, deep within myself, to their stories.

I now felt ready, and still more I felt pulled, especially
to Delos. I liked even the sound of the name, Delos,
meaning "clearly seen." The island of light, because
Apollo was born there. For centuries Ionians had built
him temples, one larger than the other. The island is still
considered sacred and is only open to visitors during early
daylight. At night it is reserved to Apollo and Artemis.

At the end of the week, Pierre and I flew first to
Mykonos from where the boat leaves daily for Delos. It was
early June, there were not yet many tourists. We rented a
scooter and crisscrossed the island, walking along beach-
es, swimming in the cold sea, looking at windmills, old
chapels, a monastery where there was one solitary nun. In
the evenings, we looked at the gold in the shop windows.

Twice we took the boat to Delos. The first time we
walked around the ruins, the sacred lake where Leto gave
birth to Apollo and Artemis, the temples. We climbed
Mont Cynthios where still longer ago, Zeus was wor-
shipped. The second time we lay down on the hillside. I
imagined the island floating, the way it did before Leto
promised that her divine son would forever shed his light
on the land.

Back in Geneva, I tried to settle down. I had difficulty
relating what had happened in Greece. I felt trapped and
uncentered. My writing seemed on hold. We were opening up our workshop to new members and I couldn't see
a new collection of writing in the near future. I was
restless.

And then I had this vivid dream.

> Pierre is sitting in front, driving a horse-drawn cart. I
> am sitting behind with two women writer friends. We are
> going to a place where the three of us will lead a work-
> shop. We have two hours to get there. Along the way we

visit a lovely village, with pastel colored houses, a square with little white lights in the trees. Everyone is having a good time, friendly, full of life.

We drive on. Pierre gets out of the carriage and goes down alongside a river. The horse continues on the path. I stay in the back with my friends. The ride is pleasant. There is some snow on the ground. I see some beautiful red berries, in groups of three or four in the snow. We keep going down rolling hills.

Pierre finally catches up with us. He is angry. Why didn't we follow him? We say we were sitting in the back.

(June 16, 1992)

The red berries reminded me of my gold pieces. The dream seemed in contrast to the period of depression I was living. In the dream I was comfortable, riding along with my two friends, first through the village with Pierre driving us, then through the rolling countryside with the horse driving us.

I took my feelings of fullness from the Greek isles and emptiness from my return, along with my dream, down to Keller.

"Fullness, emptiness. When something new is coming but not yet constellated, frustration is normal. It's time to be quiet."

"And let go." I said, "like you said last time, about the gold pieces."

"Yes," he acknowledged. "And look at what happens when you let go. The horse drives you over rolling hills, the drive is pleasant."

I saw what he was getting at. "The horse drives me without Pierre," I said. Not only had he left but he was angry that I had kept on without him.

"Yes, this time the dream seems very clear. It's time to let the horse drive you. Until now, Pierre was driving the wagon. When he leaves, you carry on. Or your instinct carries on, and it's all right. It's even pleasant."

"Like in the last dream," I said, "with the gold jewelry, Pierre disappeared."

"Precisely," said Keller, leaning forward. "Don't you see? It's a question of territory. Trying to hide your pieces of gold, going to a writers workshop, this is your territory."

I thought back over many of my dreams. I was often alone or with friends, with women, with writers, and when Pierre was there he often disappeared before the end of the dream.

"Maybe it is time to pay attention to your territory, to your independence. Do you know about the fish, called in French an *épinoche*, which is here in the Lake of Geneva?

Keller told me about the *épinoche*, a little lake fish, like the perch, about 8 cm long, but with spikes along its back. It seems that this fish has its special territory, when one *épinoche* enters the territory of another, it lowers its back spikes. It submits to the rules of the other fish. The borders are invisible, but they are respected.

"Maybe your unconscious," he said, "is telling you to establish invisible borders."

"You mean I have not yet my territory?"

"What do you think? In your dreams, you do. But do you in reality?"

We were quiet for a moment.

"I think I forgot I had spikes. I was always swimming in Pierre's territory. I came to France. I became Catholic. I married the oldest son in a family of ten children. I had six children and raised them in the language of their father. Maybe I over-adapted."

"You lowered your spikes. But they are still there."

"So now I have to raise them?"

"It might be easier to establish your own territory and put up some invisible borders. You understand, when you're on your side, you don't need him to lead the way, especially to a writers conference. You can sit back and lead yourself."

I remembered an earlier dream where again Pierre was driving me somewhere in a car and an older woman came and started to drive the car. I looked back through my dream book. It was there, six months earlier. I read it to Keller.

> Pierre and I are leaving some place, walking over snow covered roads. We find the car and Pierre starts to drive. I then see an older woman friend alongside the road. We go to get her. Pierre moves into the back and she starts to drive. She drives well.
>
> We are on a narrow road alongside a river, driving on the bank very close to the water. The road becomes a path and the car becomes a cart. The older woman is still driving us. She manages very well for the path is like flat scaffolding, full of holes.
>
> We arrive on a small island. A young child is with us, a boy. He sights a very large fish, large like a small whale, which is killed and partly out of the water. The young boy names the fish, a name which indicates its snake-like skin. "A fine eating fish," he says.
>
> (December 12, 1991)

"Superb!" said Keller.

Yes, it felt like a superb dream, yet I had not brought it to an earlier session. It had waited its time.

"What did you think about this dream?" he asked, giving me time.

"I guess not much because I didn't bring it to you. In my notes, I wondered if the woman friend was not my wiser older self."

"Why did you think of it now?

"Because again Pierre was first driving and then he gave the steering wheel to this woman."

"He moves into the back of the car and gives the steering wheel to your older Self, your ancient Self, who drives you over dangerous scaffolding, full of holes."

Yes, I could again see the flat scaffolding, like that which workmen stand on when painting a building, but the scaffolding was full of round holes.

"The old woman here represents your descent into the unconscious. The Self is driving instead of Pierre. Your own experience is steering, alongside a river, which flows downwards towards the unconscious."

So Pierre had given the wheel to my older self. I was driving the two of us. It was my territory, my country.

"Then what happens? Look at the dream. There is a new consciousness, no longer projected on Pierre. A young boy appears, he is with you on the island."

If I could take back what I had projected of my unconscious on Pierre, then there would be chance for a deeper union[95]. Instead of projection, *coniunctio.* Meeting of opposites. Birth. A young boy. This dream was exciting and timeless. It hadn't resonated earlier because I wasn't ready to let it.

"And it is not just any boy, but it is a boy who knows about fish and sights a very large one, already killed and waiting for you, as if the unconscious had prepared it."

---

95. "In general, emotional ties are very important to human beings. But they still contain projections [of one's unconscious qualities on another] and it is essential to withdraw these projections in order to attain to oneself and to objectivity." *Memories, Dreams, Reflections by C.G. Jung,* p. 328.
It is interesting to note how Jung in his paper, "Marriage as a Psychological Relationship," claimed that there can be no psychological relationship without consciousness. As long as the partners project the unconscious parts of themselves on the other, it is a marriage of two half-unconscious components. And in this sense the Self and the other are blurred. Peter O'Connor, *Understanding Jung, Understanding Yourself,* pp. 112-122.

A very large fish, waiting, half out of the water. Keller said that fish were usually associated with life and fecundity, also with spiritual life and food. And this fish had a snake-like skin. Snakes have an obscure quality, often pointing to an element of transgression.

I was familiar with the fish being a symbol of spiritual life and with the references in the New Testament, the Greek word *Icthus*, meaning fish but also its letters referring to Jesus Christ Son of God Savior, and the allusion to baptism and to the Eucharistic meal. But I questioned the snake skin pointing to transgression.

He answered with the snake in the Old Testament, tempting Eve, offering a way to knowledge, to greater consciousness. So here in my dream, the snake-like skin, which is unusual for a good eating fish, was pointing to something meaningful for the dreamer.

"Even the snake-like skin is important?"

"Exactly. It is often these small details in a dream which are important."

He went on to suggest that when I am able to assume responsibility for my territory, and no longer project on Pierre, then I will find myself transgressing some old habits, some old attitudes. "It won't necessarily be easy," he said. "You will be breaking some established conventions."

I felt Keller was right on the mark. When Pierre's territory was his family's place, I didn't have to always accompany him, even if it meant breaking some old habits. Instead of undergoing – and then resisting – the influence his family held on us at Samoëns, I could let him go alone.

And when my territory was a writers conference, Pierre didn't have to lead me. In fact he didn't have to be there at all, instead he could go down to the riverside on his own, like in my dream. And I would be free to follow my horse over the rolling hills.

Only then would Pierre and I meet as two individuals, each with our own space, each respecting the spiritual life and growth of the other.[96] I was reminded of the two solitudes of Rilke, "the love that consists in this, that two solitudes protect and border and salute each other."[97]

"And remember," added Keller, "that when you do meet, when you are together, the fish is excellent. The dream takes us right back to everyday life. It is a good fish to eat, not just to dream about."

A good eating fish with a snake-like skin.

"A superb dream," he repeated. "It takes us down into the unconscious, there is a meeting of opposites, a new consciousness is born, and then there is a banquet."

We had gone over my hour.

I was excited and with reason. The good eating fish had replaced the small spiked fish in the lake. I had gotten the message. Territories. Invisible borders. Projections. Taking the steering wheel. Letting Pierre sit back. Leading

96. M. Scott Peck wrote, "I have come to realize that it is the separateness of the partners that enriches the union... Genuine love not only respects the individuality of the other but actually seeks to cultivate it, even at the risk of separation or loss. The ultimate goal of life remains the spiritual growth of the individual." Peck, *The Road Less Traveled*, Simon & Schuster, New York, 1978, p. 168.

Peter O'Connor wrote "Unless there is a degree of separateness it is impossible, it seems, to develop a sense of oneself different and distinguishable from one's partner or others. Hence an optimal level of separateness in a marriage would be in Jung's terms a necessary precondition for consciousness." O'Connor, *Understanding Jung, Understanding Yourself*, p. 114.

97. Rilke used these words to describe the change in the love-experience that will come from giving recognition to the feminine human being, reshaping it into a relationship that is meant to be of one human being to another, "when two solitudes protect and border and salute each other." Rilke, *Letters to a Young Poet*, p. 59.

15. Pieces of Gold   165

myself. I wrote it all down. I meditated upon it. I carried it around with me.

And then I remembered that I had to let it go. An insight gained today is worth nothing tomorrow. The gold of alchemy can not be capitalized.

The red berries will disappear as the snow melts.

And the good fish is to be eaten, otherwise it will rot.

16. Beginning Again

I am sitting on a high cliff. A young child comes and sits to my right, where the ledge drops to the water. She looks about four but is smaller in size, like a baby. Another woman and her child sit to my left.

I pick up my child and put her closer, saying to the woman, "Did you see how near she was to the end of the rock?" The woman says she would let her stay there since she was sitting so comfortably on her own. I let the child move back near the edge.

She slips, falling slowly backwards, off the cliff, down into the water where she sinks and disappears out of sight. I go down slowly after her, knowing I can save her, but she comes up on her own. She looks at me, is not frightened, and starts to swim to the rocks on the shore. I watch her swim on her own. I am not worried. It is all peaceful.

(September 28, 1992)

This was the dream I had on the morning of my fifty-eighth birthday. I had gone to sleep, hoping to have a birthday dream and hoping to remember it. I had been in analysis one year, from September 91 to September 92. I thought a special dream might mark the date.

At first I found the contents of this dream contradictory, the child sitting alone, my wanting to hold her closer, the woman next to me telling me not to, the child falling, my wanting to save her, finally the child swimming on her own. Yet as I thought about it, and saw again the child falling into the water, sinking, and then swimming to shore on her own, it started to answer my birthday hopes.

Here was my child, my new awareness, my creative side, sitting comfortably on the edge of a cliff. Probably if I had not pulled her closer, if my negative mothering had not overprotected her, she would still be comfortable there. Instead she fell and sank into the water. Again I was ready to save her. But no, she was able to swim on her own. She looked at me and started off swimming alone.

I remembered the initiatory dream of my analysis which was the dream I first read to Keller[98]. Again there had been a little girl. Again she had fallen over the cliff. But she had fallen because she was holding my hand. We had fallen together. The water was dark and the little girl was unable to swim alone. I had shouted for help. It was not a peaceful dream. The water was dark and murky, the tides were pushing me out. I kept trying to swim back to shore while holding the little girl.

Now after one year of analysis, I was ready in my dream to let the little girl swim peacefully on her own. I even had a strong voice to my left, telling me to let her be. "She was sitting there so comfortably on her own." It could be my voice. I could be both women. I could be also the little child. My creativity was ready to go ahead on its own – if I would let it – to swim back to the shoreline, the threshold of new consciousness.

I took the dream to Keller. It was the second session since the summer break. I had been back to the States in August, teaching at another writers workshop and visiting with my mother. My "American" dreams had been all about leaving someplace. I was moving on. I was preparing for a voyage, alone, without my children and my husband. Keller had reminded me that most likely this voyage would be interior. I did not have to travel far away, leaving husband and children and friends. I could travel

98. See chapter 2, Murky Water

within. I could move away from my traditional roles and find a new way of acting, a new autonomy, while living here at home in Geneva.

Now I brought my birthday dream.

"Yes," he said, as I explained how I saw this dream, "it is a good anniversary dream, for both your birthday and for one year of analysis. It shows the permanent paradox of each individuation process."

"Paradox?"

"The dialectic between the doing and the non-doing[99], between being conscious and being not conscious."

"But the child was able to swim on her own. I didn't have to go down into the water. I didn't have to do anything." I found myself defending the passive role, the one which I was trying to learn.

"How do you know? In your dream, you did go. And the child came up, looked at you, and then swam. Perhaps if you had not gone, if she had not seen you, she would have been afraid and unable to swim."

He explained. We can be conscious and not conscious at the same time. Active and passive. It was good to let her sit near the edge, it was good to go after her. It was good to let her swim alone, it was good to stay near and watch her. Doing, non-doing.

Keller reminded me of one of the few books which he had recommended during the past year. Usually he suggested that I could read less, that I could stop trying to

99. "The art of letting things happen, action through non-action, letting go of oneself, as taught by Meister Eckhart, became for me the key opening the door to the way. We must be able to let things happen in the psyche. For us, this actually is an art of which few people know anything. Consciousness is forever interfering, helping, correcting, and negating, and never leaving the simple growth of the psychic processes in peace." C.G. Jung, Commentary on Taoist text. *The Secret of The Golden Flower*, translated by Richard Wilhelm, Harcourt Brace Jovanovich, New York, 1962, p. 93.

understand all the time, reminding me that I couldn't hold on to my frogs. But three or four times, he had suggested I read something. And twice it was the same book, *Zen Mind, Beginner's Mind*, by Shunryu Suzuki. I had bought the book and read it. It was not my way of thinking. It was all about not understanding.

Zen Mind, Beginner's Mind originated from a series of talks given by Suzuki-roshi to the Zen Center at San Francisco. Beginner's mind is the open mind, the attitude that includes both doubt and possibility, the ability to see things always as fresh and new.

> "We must have beginner's mind, free from possessing anything, a mind that knows everything is in flowing change. Nothing exists but momentarily in its present form and color. One thing flows into another and cannot be grasped. Before the rain stops we hear a bird. Even under the heavy snow we see snowdrops and some new growth."[100]

My dream was pointing to beginner's mind. I was to simply live without questioning my life, my purpose. "It's like putting a horse," Suzuki once said, "on top of a horse and then climbing on and trying to ride. Riding a horse by itself is hard enough. Why add another horse? Then it's impossible."

Our questions, Keller said, are that extra horse. All we have to do is live our lives and be ourselves every moment.

My constant questioning, wanting to understand, wanting to do better, was indeed like putting one horse on top of another and trying to ride. And once more I was always

100. Shunryu Suzuki, *Zen Mind, Beginner's Mind*, Weatherhill, New York & Japan, 1991, p. 138. Zen mind leads to perfect composure. "When you have something in your consciousness you do not have perfect composure. The best way towards perfect composure is to forget everything. Then your mind is calm, and it is wide and clear enough to see and feel things as they are without any effort." p. 128.

ready to blame myself – even on top of two horses – for not being able to ride faster.

"Stop always censuring yourself," said Keller. "It's all right to let the child be and it's all right to go after her."

I listened to him.

"This is beginner's mind, this is your child, your new consciousness, doing and not doing."

He described the old fisherman, sitting on the pier, quietly holding his pole. It looks like he's doing nothing. But he's fishing.

"This is the interior attitude that you've been traveling to through your last dreams, letting go, being yourself."

My traveling had seemed so often in circles, back again to the green frogs, back to the maple tree, to the cat at the door. the witch in the backyard. Yet through it all there was this pattern of letting go, of moving on, of being myself.

I thought of the ancient manuscript which is called a meander, where the scrolls and circles seem fragmented and repetitive, but where in reality they follow a meandering pattern coming back to something already seen and then disappearing into something new. Von Franz used this example of the meander as an image of the process of individuation[101]. Had I not been discovering and rediscovering this pattern throughout the year of dreams and analysis?

I went home slowly, crossing the bridge and driving along the lake. The plane trees lining the quay were still

---

101. "Thus our dream life creates a meandering pattern in which individual strands or tendencies become visible, then vanish, then return again. If one watches this meandering design over a long period of time, one can observe a sort of hidden regulating or directing tendency at work, creating a slow imperceptible process of psychic growth – the process of individuation." von Franz, *Man and His Symbols*, p. 161.

immense with green leaves. I looked at them with beginner's mind. Soon the leaves would turn bright yellow and then they would fall to the dark ground. Everything is cyclical.[102]

I saw all of creation like one giant tree, reaching with its roots downward to our common source, to God[103], to the collective unconscious, to the Tao – to that something that cannot be told[104]. I saw it reaching outward and upwards with its branches to include all of the universe. I experienced a sense of oneness, an awareness of being part of a whole. My own individual identity seemed less real than my participation in something larger, something universal. The "I" was no longer there and yet I was more alive than ever.

Autumn and then winter were ahead of me. Another year. I was starting anew. A second year of analysis, every

102. Jean Shinoda Bolen explains that this living with the seasons, is following the inner Tao path, in which our experience of time is different. "We have only one word for time; the Greeks had two... One was *kronos*, time as we usually watch it, measured time passing... The second was *kairos*, participation in time, time that so engrosses us we lose track of time, timeless time... time when we feel 'one with,' rather than separate from, the Self, the Tao, the love that connects us to others." Bolen, *The Tao of Psychology*, p. 93.

103. Jung near the end of his life wrote to Laurens van der Post "I cannot define for you what God is, I can only tell you that my work as a natural scientist has established empirically that the pattern which men call God exists in every man, and that this pattern has at its disposal the greatest transformative energies of life." Laurens van der Post, *Yet Being Someone Other*, Penguin Books, London, 1987, p. 351.

Thomas Merton in an essay, "The New Consciousness" wrote, "The self is not its own center and does not orbit around itself; it is centered on God, the one center of all, which is 'everywhere and nowhere,' in whom all are encountered, from whom all proceed." Merton, *Zen and the Birds of Appetite*, New Directions Books, New York, 1968, p. 24.

104. "The Tao that can be told is not the eternal Tao. The name that can be named is not the eternal name." (Ch. 1) So begins the *Tao Te Ching*, the ancient Taoist text ascribed to Lao Tsu, keeper of the imperial archives at the ancient capital of Loyang, 2500 years ago.

other week, a slower pace. Doing and non-doing. Autumn and letting go. Being still through winter, finding the crack in the dark. Then spring and rebirth. Seeing with my eyes closed.

Beginning again.

> "For everything there is a season, and
> a time for every matter under heaven:
> a time to be born, and a time to die;
> a time to plant, and a time to pluck up what is planted...
> a time to weep, and a time to laugh;
> a time to mourn, and a time to dance
> a time to cast away stones, and a time to gather stones
> together..."
>
>   Ecclesiastes 3: 1-4 [105]

---

105. For this quotation, I have gone back to The Revised Standard Version of *The Holy Bible*, (Thomas Nelson & Sons, New York, 1953) which is a revision of the King James Version, the Bible of my youth.

September plane trees are still immense with leaves.
(Quai de Genève, Switzerland)

Bibliography

Aristophanes, *Four Plays*, First Meridian Classic Printing, Penguin Books, Canada 1984.

Begg, Ean, *The Cult of the Black Virgin*, Arkana, Penguin Group, London, 1985.

Bly, Robert, *A Little Book on the Human Shadow*, Harper San Francisco, 1988.

Bolen, Jean Shinoda, *The Tao of Psychology*, Harper & Row, San Francisco, 1979.

Goddesses in Everywoman, Harper and Row, New York, 1985.

Gods in Everyman, Harper and Row, New York, 1989.

Bosnak, Robert, *A Little Course in Dreams*, Shambhala, Boston, 1988.

Dourley, John, *The Illness That We Are*, Inner City Books, Toronto, 1984.

Campbell, Joseph, *Myths to Live By*, Bantam Books, New York, 1972.

Edinger, Edward, *The Creation of Consciousness*, Inner City Books, Toronto, 1984.

Goethe's Faust, Inner City Books, Toronto, 1991.

Eliot, T.S, *Four Quartets*, Harcourt, Brace & Company, New York, 1943.

Estés, Clarissa Pinkola, *Women Who Run With the Wolves*, Ballantine Books, New York, 1992.

Fox, Matthew, *Original Blessing*, Bear & Company, Santa Fe, 1983.

Goethe, Johann Wolfgang von, *Faust*, New Translation by Walter Arndt, Norton Critical Edition, W.W. Norton & Company, New York, 1976.

Grimm, J.L.K., Grimm, W.K., *Grimms' Tales For Young and Old*, translated by Ralph Manheim, Anchors Books, Doubleday, New York, 1983.

Gustafson, Fred, *The Black Madonna*, Sigo Press, Boston, 1990.

Hall, James, *Jungian Dream Interpretation*, Inner City Books, Toronto, 1983.

Hamilton, Edith, *Mythology*, New American Library, New York, 1973.

Heilbrun, Carolyn, *Writing a Woman's Life*, Ballantine Books, New York, 1988.

Hillman, James, *The Dream and the Underworld*, Harper & Row, New York, 1979.

Hoffman, Eva, *Lost in Translation*, Penguin Books, New York, 1989.

Jaffé, Aniela, "Symbolism in the Visual Arts," *Man And His Symbols*, Pan Books, London, 1964.

Jewett, Julia, "Womansoul: A Feminine Corrective to Christian Imagery," *Jung's Challenge to Contemporary Religion*, edited by Murray Stein, Robert Moore, Chiron Publications, Wilmette, 1987.

Johnson, Robert, *Owning Your Own Shadow*, Harper, San Francisco, 1990.

She, Harper Row, New York, 1989.

Ecstasy, Harper, San Francisco, 1987.

We, Harper, San Francisco, 1983.

Jung, C.G., *The Portable Jung*, edited by Joseph Campbell, Penguin Books, New York, 1987. Selections in this volume come from the Collected Works of Carl G. Jung (Translated by R.F.C. Hull, Bollingen Series XX, Princeton University Press) 1, 3, 5, 6, 7, 8, 9, 12, 14, plus "On Synchronicity," "Answer to Job."

Memories, Dreams, Reflections by C.G. Jung, recorded and edited by Aniela Jaffé, Flamingo, London, 1983.

Man And His Symbols, conceived and edited by Carl Jung, with contributions from Joseph L. Henderson, M.-L. von Franz, Aniela Jaffé, Jolande Jacobi, Pan Books Ltd, London, 1978.

The Undiscovered Self, Little Brown Company, Boston, 1958.

Jung, Emma, *The Grail Legend*, (with Marie-Louise von Franz)
    Sigo Press, Boston, 1986

Merton, Thomas, *Selected Poems of Thomas Merton*, New
    Directions Books, New York City, 1967.
    Zen and the Birds of Appetite, New Directions Books, New
    York City, 1968.

Moore, Robert, "Ritual Process, Initiation, and Contemporary
    Religion," *Jung's Challenge to Contemporary Religion*,
    Chiron Publications, Illinois, 1987.

Moore, Thomas, *Care of the Soul*, Harper Collins, New York,
    1992.

Murdock, Maureen, *The Heroine's Journey*, Shambhala, Boston,
    1990.

O'Connor, Peter, *Understanding Jung, Understanding Yourself*,
    Paulist Press, New York, 1985.

Peck, M. Scott, *The Road Less Traveled*, Simon & Shuster, New
    York, 1978.

Perera, Sylvia, *Descent to the Goddess*, Inner City Books, Toronto,
    1981.

Rilke, Rainer Maria, *Letters to a Young Poet*, W.W. Norton, New
    York, 1962.

Sarton, May, *Journal of a Solitude*, Norton, New York, 1977.

Singer, June, *Androgyny*, Doubleday, New York, 1976.
    Seeing Through the Visible World, Harper & Row, San
    Francisco, 1990.

Sternberg, Janet, *The Writer on Her Work*, Volume II, W.W.
    Norton, New York, 1991.

Suzuki, Shunryu, *Zen Mind, Beginner's Mind*, Weatherhill, New
    York & Japan, 1991.

Teilhard de Chardin, *Hymn of the Universe*, Harper & Row, New
    York, 1965.

Ueland, Brenda, *If You Want to Write*, Graywolf Press, Saint Paul
    1987.

Upjohn, Sheila, *In Search of Julian of Norwich*, Darton, Longsman
    & Todd, London, 1989.

van der Post, Laurens, *Jung and the Story of Our Time*, Penguin
    Books, London, 1976.
    Yet Being Someone Other, Penguin Books, London, 1987.

von Franz, Marie-Louise, *Shadow and Evil in Fairy Tales*, Spring
    Publications, Dallas, 1974.

    The Grail Legend (with Emma Jung), Sigo Press, Boston,
    1986.

    Interpretation of Fairy Tales, Spring Publications, New York,
    1970.

    Alchemy, An Introduction to the Symbolism and the
    Psychology, Inner City Books, Toronto, 1980.

Welch, John, *Spiritual Pilgrims*, Carl Jung and Teresa of Avila,
    Paulist Press, New York, 1982.

Woodman, Marion, *Addiction To Perfection*, Inner City Books,
    Toronto, 1982.

    Leaving My Father's House, Shambhala, Boston, 1993.

Woolf, Virginia, *A Room of One's Own*, Harcourt Brace
    Jovanovich, New York, 1989.

Dictionary of Symbols, Tom Chetwynd, Paladin, Grafton Books,
    London, 1982.

Dictionnaire des Symboles, Jean Chevalier, Alain Gheerbrant,
    Editions Robert Laffont / Jupiter, Paris, 1992.

Holy Bible, Revised Standard Edition, Thomas Nelson and Sons,
    New York, 1953.

I Ching or Book of Changes, Richard Wilhelm Translation,
    Foreword by C.G. Jung, Arkana, Penguin Group,
    London, 1983.

Jerusalem Bible, Popular Edition, Darton, Longman & Todd,
    London, 1974.

Modern American Poetry, Modern British Poetry, edited by Louis
    Untermeyer, Harcourt Brace & Company, New York,
    1950.

Secret of the Golden Flower, A Chinese Book of Life, translated and
    explained by Richard Wilhelm, Commentary by C.G.
    Jung, Harcourt Brace Jovanovich, New York, 1962.

Tao Te Ching, Lao Tsu, Translated by Gia-Fu & Jane English,
    Introduction by Jacob Needleman, Vintage Books, 1989.

Illustrations and Credits

Index

Alan McGlashan
Gravity and Levity
The Philosophy of Paradox
162 pages
This book heralds a breakthrough in human imagination, not a breakthrough that may take place in the future, far or near, but one that has already occurred – only we may not have noticed it. Life, as the author shows, is open-ended and full of paradoxes. Its principles cannot be understood by logic and causal reasoning. We can only come to terms with life if we accept that

there is no final answer to it and that adjusting to life's natural rhythm is the key to finding release from the horrors and problems around us.

TALKING WITH ANGELS Budaliget 1943
A document transcribed by Gitta Mallasz
474 pages, revised second edition
Budaliget 1943: A small village on the edge of Budapest. Three young women and a man, artists and close friends are gathered together in the uneasy days before Hitler's armies would destroy the world as they knew it. Seeking spiritual knowledge, and anticipating the horrors of Nazi-occupied Hungary, they met regularly to discuss how to find their own inner paths to enlightenment.
For 17 months, with the world locked in a deadly struggle for survival, the four friends meet every week with the spiritual beings they come to call their "angels"; Gitta Mallasz takes notes, the protocols which form this book, along with her commentary. The angels' message of personal responsibility is as meaningful and as urgent today as it was for its initial recipients half a century ago.

I am deeply touched by the dialogues with the angels.
Yehudi Menuhin

I could read it over and over again and never get tired of it.
Thank you, thank you, thank you for sharing this book with me.
Elisabeth Kübler-Ross

Hayao Kawai
Dreams, Myths and Fairy Tales in Japan

The well-known Japanese author, university professor and Zürich-trained Jungian analyst, Hayao Kawai, presents here the long-awaited second of his works in English. Originally presented as lectures at the historic Eranos Conferences in Ascona, this book describes five Japanese fairy tales, insightfully examined from Eastern and Western vantage points by an author intimately familiar with both. (158 pages, illustrated)

Rainer Maria Rilke
Duino Elegies

Translated by David Oswald

The *Duino Elegies* are one of the twentieth century's great works of art. In the space of ten elegies, presented here in a bilingual edition, an impassioned voice struggles to find an answer to what it means to be human in a world torn by modern consciousness. (128 pages)

C.A. Meier
Personality

The Individuation Process
in the Light of C.G. Jung's Typology

Carl Gustav Jung never produced a systematic treatment of his own work – he was always moving forward. His assistant-of-many-decades, Carl Alfred Meier, made it his life-task to gather and present in detail the various aspects of Jung's far-reaching discoveries. This final volume of Meier's work addresses the human personality in its encounters between consciousness and the unconscious, a process referred to as *individuation*. In describing such encounters, the author extensively explains the notion of Jung's *psychological types*. (192 pages)

Susan Bach
LIFE PAINTS ITS OWN SPAN
On the Significance of Spontaneous
Paintings by Severely Ill Children
with over 200 color illustrations
Part I (Text): 208 pages,
part II (Pictures): 56 pp., 240 x 200 mm

SUSAN BACH

LIFE PAINTS ITS OWN SPAN

ON THE SIGNIFICANCE
OF SPONTANEOUS PICTURES
BY SEVERELY ILL CHILDREN

Life Paints its own Span with over
200 color reproductions is a com-
prehensive exposition of Susan
Bach's original approach to the
physical and psychospiritual evalu-
ation of spontaneous paintings and
drawings by severely ill patients. At the same time, this work is a
moving record of Susan Bach's own journey of discovery.

Forthcoming:

The Rock Rabbit
and the Rainbow
A Tribute to
Laurens van der Post

A Festschrift for Laurens van der Post
The Rock Rabbit and the Rainbow
edited by Robert Hinshaw
Authors from around the world have
combined their talents in a tribute honor-
ing this one-of-a-kind writer, soldier and
statesman, a man of his time. Contributions include: Joseph Henderson: "The
Splendor of the Sun"; Alan McGlashan:
"How to be Haveable"; Ian Player: "My
Friend Nkunzimlanga"; Jean-Marc Pot-
tiez: "Rainbow Rhapsody"; T.C. Robert-
son: "A Triad of Landscapes – a Day in
the Veld with Laurens"; and numerous
other essays and works by Aniela Jaffé,
Jonathan Stedall, Harry Wilmer, Jo
Wheelright, C.A. Meier and many others.
(ca. 240 pages, illustrated)

ENGLISH PUBLICATIONS BY *DAIMON*

Susan Bach – *Life Paints its Own Span*
E.A. Bennet – *Meetings with Jung*
George Czuczka – *Imprints of the Future*
Heinrich Karl Fierz – *Jungian Psychiatry*
von Franz / Frey-Rohn / Jaffé – *What is Death?*
Liliane Frey-Rohn – *Friedrich Nietzsche*
Yael Haft – *Hands: Archetypal Chirology*
Siegmund Hurwitz – *Lilith, the first Eve*
Aniela Jaffé   – *The Myth of Meaning*
                    – *Was C.G. Jung a Mystic?*
                    – *From the Life und Work of C.G. Jung*
                    – *Death Dreams and Ghosts*
Verena Kast   – *A Time to Mourn*
                    – *Sisyphus*
Hayao Kawai – *Dreams, Myths and Fairy Tales in Japan*
James Kirsch   – *The Reluctant Prophet*
Rivkah Schärf Kluger   – *The Gilgamesh Epic*
Rafael López-Pedraza   – *Hermes and his Children*
                        – *Cultural Anxiety*
Alan McGlashan – *The Savage and Beautiful Country*
                    – *Gravity and Levity*
Gitta Mallasz (Transcription) – *Talking with Angels*
C.A. Meier   – *Healing Dream and Ritual*
                    – *A Testament to the Wilderness*
Laurens van der Post – *A «Festschrift»*
R.M. Rilke – *Duino Elegies*
Ann Ulanov – *The Wizards' Gate*

Jungian Congress Papers:
Jerusalem 1983 – *Symbolic and Clinical Approaches*
Berlin 1986 – *Archetype of Shadow in a Split World*
Paris 1989 – *Dynamics in Relationship*
Chicago 1992 – *The Transcendent Function*

Available from your bookstore or from our distributors:

In the United States:

Atrium Publishers Group
P.O. Box 108
Lower Lake, CA 95457
Tel. (707) 995 3906
Fax: (707) 995 1814

Chiron Publications
400 Linden Avenue
Wilmette, IL 60091
Tel. (708) 256 7551
Fax: (708) 256 2202

In Great Britain:

Airlift Book Company
26-28 Eden Grove
London N7 8EF, England
Tel. (607) 5792 and 5798
Fax (607) 6714

Worldwide: Daimon Verlag
            Hauptstrasse 85
            CH-8840 Einsiedeln Switzerland
            Tel. (41)(55) 532266
            Fax (41)(55) 532231   *Write for our complete catalog!*